MORE Bible PUZZLES

PEOPLE OF THE BIBLE

AGES 8 & UP

For information regarding the CPSIA on this printed material call:
203-595-3636 and provide reference # LANC-315751

rainbowpublishers®

www.RainbowPublishers.com

MORE Bible PUZZLES

PEOPLE OF THE BIBLE

AGES 8 & UP

Margie Harding

Lovingly dedicated to my children: Tammy, Shannon, Beth, Chad and Dave.

MORE BIBLE PUZZLES: PEOPLE OF THE BIBLE
©2012 by Rainbow Publishers, fourth printing
ISBN 10: 1-58411-052-X
ISBN 13: 978-1-58411-052-1
Rainbow reorder# RB38433
RELIGION / Christian Ministry / Children

Rainbow Publishers
P.O. Box 261129
San Diego, CA 92196
www.RainbowPublishers.com

Interior Illustrators: Chuck Galey and Aline Heiser

Scriptures are from the *Holy Bible: New International Version* (North American Edition), ©1973, 1978, 1984 by the International Bible Society. Used by permission of Zondervan Bible Publishers.

Printed in the United States of America

contents

introduction

*M*ore Bible Puzzles: *People of the Bible* is a collection of puzzles based on favorite stories of people throughout the Bible, both Old and New Testaments. The puzzles – with their unique challenges – are an enjoyable way to learn more about important events in the Bible. These puzzles make a good teaching resource. They provide an incentive for children or adults to study God's Word. And they are great for individual enjoyment, too!

Disobedience
Genesis 3:17-19

The Bible tells how sin entered the world through Adam because he disobeyed God. Paul discusses the spiritual connection between Adam and someone else in Romans 5:12-21. Use the letters in "disobedience" to fill in the missing letters in the Scripture from Genesis 3:17b-19. Then use the letters above the numbers to find the spiritual connection Paul discusses in Romans 5:12-21.

"_ur___ _s th_ gr_u__ ___au__ _f y_u;
 8   17   22   24   6

thr_u gh pa___ful t__l y_u w_ll _at _f _t all
 21   5   27

th_ _ay_ _f y_ur l_f_. _t w_ll pr___u__
18   20   15   3

th_r__ an_ th__tl__ f_r y_u, a__ y_u
11   23   13   10

w_ll _at th_ pla_t_ _f th_ f__l. _y th_
                    9   2   25

_w_at _f y_ur _r_w y_u w_ll _at y_ur f___
              1   14

u_t_l y_u r_tur_ t_ th_ gr_u__, _____
          16   7   28

fr_m _t y_u w_r_ tak__; f_r _u_t y_u ar_
19   29   12   26

a__ t_ _u_t y_u w_ll r_tur_."   – Genesis 3:17b-19
    4

___ ___ ___ ___ ___ ___ ___ ___ ___   ___ ___ ___   ___ ___ ___ ___
 1   2   3   4   5   6   7   8   9   10 11 12   13 14 15 16

___ ___ ___ ___ ___ ___ ___   ___ ___ ___ ___ ___ ___   (from Romans 5:12-21)
17 18 19 20 21 22 23   24 25 26 27 28 29

9

Disobedience

Answer

"Curs e d is the ground because of you;
8   17   22   24   6

through painful to il you will eat of it all
21   5   27

the days of your life. It will produce
18   20   15   3

thorns and thistles for you, and you
11   23   13   10

will eat the plants of the field. By the
                                  9   2   25

sweat of your brow you will eat your food
                  1   14

until you return to the ground, since
16   7   28

from it you were taken; for dust you are
19   29   12   26

and to dust you will return." – Genesis 3:17b-19
       4

O b e d i e n c e   a n d   l i f e
1 2 3 4 5 6 7 8 9 10 11 12 13 14 15 16

t h r o u g h   C h r i s t (from Romans 5:12-21)
17 18 19 20 21 22 23 24 25 26 27 28 29

A Pleasing Sacrifice
Genesis 4:1-8

Cain and Abel both brought offerings to the Lord. God rejected Cain's offering, but He accepted Abel's. The difference was that Abel made a faith offering and God was pleased with him. Find the missing number in each group to break the code to find out what offering Abel made to God.

2, 4, __, 8 = H   9, __, 27, 36 = E   7, __, 13, 16 = I   1, __, 15, 22 = A

1, __, 3, 4 = B   4, 8, __, 16 = P   3, __, 5, 6 = R   11, __, 15, 17 = M

5, 10, 15, __ = O   11, 22, __, 44 = F   1, __, 5, 7 = K   7, __, 21, 28 = N

3, 6, __, 12 = C   5, 6, __, 8 = T   0, __, 10, 15 = L   5, 10, __, 20 = U

20, __, 24, 26 = S   8, __, 14, 17 = G

__ __ __ __   __ __ __ __ __ __ __   __ __ __
8   2   18   5   2   4   20   15   11   6   7   33   8   7

__ __ __ __ __ __ __ __   __ __ __ __   __ __ __ __
12   20   4   7   10   20   14   22   33   4   20   13   22   20   13   18

__ __   __ __ __   __ __ __ __ __ __ __ __ __
20   33   7   6   18   33   10   4   22   7   2   20   4   14

__ __   __ __ __   __ __ __ __ __.   **(from Genesis 4:4)**
20   33   6   10   22   33   5   20   9   3

A Pleasing Sacrifice

Answer

2, 4, 6, 8 = H   9, 18, 27, 36 = E   7, 10, 13, 16 = I   1, 8, 15, 22 = A

1, 2, 3, 4 = B   4, 8, 12, 16 = P   3, 4, 5, 6 = R   11, 13, 15, 17 = M

5, 10, 15, 20 = O   11, 22, 33, 44 = F   1, 3, 5, 7 = K   7, 14, 21, 28 = N

3, 6, 9, 12 = C   5, 6, 7, 8 = T   0, 5, 10, 15 = L   5, 10, 15, 20 = U

20, 22, 24, 26 = S   8, 11, 14, 17 = G

A b e l   b r o u g h t   f a t
8 2 18 5   2 4 20 15 11 6 7   33 8 7

p o r t i o n s   f r o m   s o m e
12 20 4 7 10 20 14 22   33 4 20 13   22 20 13 18

o f   t h e   f i r s t b o r n
20 33   7 6 18   33 10 4 22 7 2 20 4 14

o f   h i s   f l o c k.   (from Genesis 4:4)
20 33   6 10 22   33 5 20 9 3

12

A Major Project
Genesis 6:9-8:22

The Bible gives a lot of numbers about Noah's ark and all of the events surrounding the Flood. God told Noah to build an ark with specific measurements. Then it rained a specific number of days and the earth was covered with water for a certain number of days. Do the math to find these numbers that are recorded in Genesis 6. (Remember, each function in the problem is figured from its previous total!)

1. **How long was the ark?** $75 \times 2 + 69 \div 3 \times 3 + 54 - 73 + 270 - 20 =$ _____

2. **How wide was the ark?** $56 - 23 \times 3 - 47 \times 2 - 29 =$ _____

3. **How tall was the ark?** $15 \times 6 \div 5 + 22 - 15 \times 3 - 30 =$ _____

4. **How many doors were in the ark?** $492 - 92 \times 2 - 798 - 1 =$ _____

5. **How many floors were in the ark?** $15 \times 3 \div 3 + 15 \div 3 - 7 =$ _____

6. **How many of each kind of animal did Noah take into the ark?**

   $214 \div 2 + 3 \div 5 - 20 =$ _____

7. **How old was Noah when the rain came?** $795 - 85 \div 5 \times 8 - 600 + 64 =$ _____

8. **How many days did the rain fall?** $92 \times 2 \div 4 \div 2 + 17 =$ _____

9. **How many nights did it rain?** $12 \times 6 \div 3 \times 2 - 8 =$ _____

10. **The water rose how high above the mountain peaks?**

    $450 - 325 \div 5 \times 2 - 35 + 5 =$ _____

11. **The earth was flooded how many days?** $695 - 150 \div 5 + 45 - 4 =$ _____

12. **Noah released a raven how many days after the rain stopped?**

    $382 \times 2 \div 4 - 31 \div 4 =$ _____

13. **Noah released a dove how many days after he released the raven?**

    $15 \times 6 \div 3 - 27 + 4 =$ _____

14. **How many more days passed before Noah released the dove for the trip from which it did not return, signifying Noah could leave the ark?**

    $139 - 42 \times 3 - 189 \div 6 - 10 =$ _____

(from Genesis 6-8)

A Major Project

Answer

1. **How long was the ark?** 75 x 2 + 69 ÷ 3 x 3 + 54 - 73 + 270 - 20 = <u>450 feet</u>

2. **How wide was the ark?** 56 - 23 x 3 - 47 x 2 - 29 = <u>75 feet</u>

3. **How tall was the ark?** 15 x 6 ÷ 5 + 22 - 15 x 3 - 30 = <u>45 feet</u>

4. **How many doors were in the ark?** 492 - 92 x 2 - 798 -1 = <u>1 door in the side</u>

5. **How many floors were in the ark?** 15 x 3 ÷ 3 + 15 ÷ 3 - 7 = <u>3 floors: lower, middle and upper deck</u>

6. **How many of each kind of animal did Noah take into the ark?** 214 ÷ 2 + 3 ÷ 5 - 20 = <u>2</u>

7. **How old was Noah when the rain came?** 795 - 85 ÷ 5 x 8 - 600 + 64 = <u>600 years old</u>

8. **How many days did the rain fall?** 92 x 2 ÷ 4 ÷ 2 + 17 = <u>40 days</u>

9. **How many nights did it rain?** 12 x 6 ÷ 3 x 2 - 8 = <u>40 nights</u>

10. **The water rose how high above the mountain peaks?** 450 - 325 ÷ 5 x 2 - 35 + 5 = <u>20 feet</u>

11. **The earth was flooded how many days?** 695 - 150 ÷ 5 + 45 - 4 = <u>150 days</u>

12. **Noah released a raven how many days after the rain stopped?** 382 x 2 ÷ 4 - 31 ÷ 4 = <u>40 days</u>

13. **Noah released a dove how many days after he released the raven?** 15 x 6 ÷ 3 - 27 + 4 = <u>7 days</u>

14. **How many more days passed before Noah released the dove for the trip from which it did not return, signifying Noah could leave the ark?** 139 - 42 x 3 - 189 ÷ 6 - 10 = <u>7 days</u>

(from Genesis 6-8)

Time to Leave
Genesis 12:1,4

God called Abram to do something special, yet difficult. Abram had faith that God knew what was best. When it was time, Abram followed God's instructions. Use the clock to decode God's instructions and how Abram responded. Then use the code to see how Abram's response is a challenge to all believers.

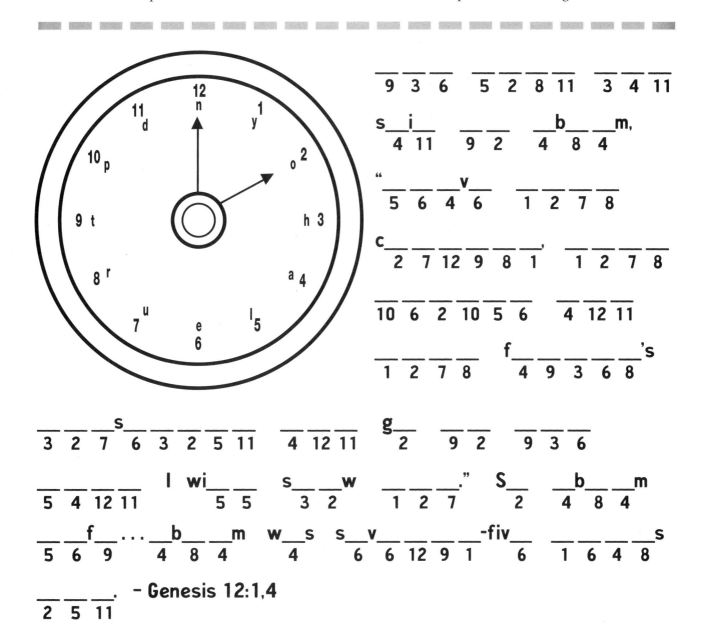

$\overline{9}\ \overline{3}\ \overline{6}\quad \overline{5}\ \overline{2}\ \overline{8}\ \overline{11}\quad \overline{3}\ \overline{4}\ \overline{11}$

s$\overline{}$i$\overline{}$ $\overline{}\overline{}$ $\overline{}$b$\overline{}$ $\overline{}$m,
$\quad \overline{4}\ \overline{11}\quad \overline{9}\ \overline{2}\quad \overline{4}\ \overline{8}\ \overline{4}$

" $\overline{}\ \overline{}\ \overline{}v\overline{}$ $\overline{}\ \overline{}\ \overline{}\ \overline{}$
$\overline{5}\ \overline{6}\ \overline{4}\ \overline{6}\quad \overline{1}\ \overline{2}\ \overline{7}\ \overline{8}$

c$\overline{}\ \overline{}\ \overline{}\ \overline{}\ \overline{}\ \overline{}$, $\overline{}\ \overline{}\ \overline{}\ \overline{}$
$\overline{2}\ \overline{7}\ \overline{12}\ \overline{9}\ \overline{8}\ \overline{1}\quad \overline{1}\ \overline{2}\ \overline{7}\ \overline{8}$

$\overline{10}\ \overline{6}\ \overline{2}\ \overline{10}\ \overline{5}\ \overline{6}\quad \overline{4}\ \overline{12}\ \overline{11}$

$\overline{}\ \overline{}\ \overline{}\ \overline{}$ f$\overline{}\ \overline{}\ \overline{}\ \overline{}\ \overline{}$'s
$\overline{1}\ \overline{2}\ \overline{7}\ \overline{8}\quad\ \overline{4}\ \overline{9}\ \overline{3}\ \overline{6}\ \overline{8}$

$\overline{}\ \overline{}\ \overline{}s\overline{}\ \overline{}\ \overline{}\ \overline{}\ \overline{}$ $\overline{}\ \overline{}\ \overline{}$ g$\overline{}$ $\overline{}\ \overline{}$ $\overline{}\ \overline{}\ \overline{}$
$\overline{3}\ \overline{2}\ \overline{7}\ \overline{6}\ \overline{3}\ \overline{2}\ \overline{5}\ \overline{11}\quad \overline{4}\ \overline{12}\ \overline{11}\quad\ \overline{2}\quad \overline{9}\ \overline{2}\quad \overline{9}\ \overline{3}\ \overline{6}$

$\overline{}\ \overline{}\ \overline{}\ \overline{}$ I wi$\overline{}\ \overline{}$ s$\overline{}\ \overline{}$w $\overline{}\ \overline{}\ \overline{}$." S$\overline{}$ $\overline{}$b$\overline{}\ \overline{}$m
$\overline{5}\ \overline{4}\ \overline{12}\ \overline{11}\quad\ \ \overline{5}\ \overline{5}\quad \overline{3}\ \overline{2}\quad \overline{1}\ \overline{2}\ \overline{7}\quad \overline{2}\quad \overline{4}\ \overline{8}\ \overline{4}$

$\overline{}\ \overline{}f\overline{}$ . . . $\overline{}$b$\overline{}\ \overline{}$m w$\overline{}$s s$\overline{}v\overline{}\ \overline{}\ \overline{}\ \overline{}$-fiv$\overline{}$ $\overline{}\ \overline{}\ \overline{}\ \overline{}$s
$\overline{5}\ \overline{6}\ \overline{9}\quad\ \overline{4}\ \overline{8}\ \overline{4}\quad \overline{4}\quad \overline{6}\ \overline{6}\ \overline{12}\ \overline{9}\ \overline{1}\quad \overline{6}\quad \overline{1}\ \overline{6}\ \overline{4}\ \overline{8}$

$\overline{}\ \overline{}\ \overline{}$. – Genesis 12:1,4
$\overline{2}\ \overline{5}\ \overline{11}$

Challenge:

$\overline{}\ \overline{}$w c$\overline{}\ \overline{}$ I f$\overline{}\ \overline{}\ \overline{}\ \overline{}\ \overline{}$w C$\overline{}\ \overline{}is\overline{}$'s c$\overline{}\ \overline{}\ \overline{}$?
$\overline{3}\ \overline{2}\quad \overline{4}\ \overline{12}\quad\ \overline{2}\ \overline{5}\ \overline{5}\ \overline{2}\quad \overline{3}\ \overline{8}\ \overline{9}\quad \overline{4}\ \overline{5}\ \overline{5}$

15

Time to Leave

Answer

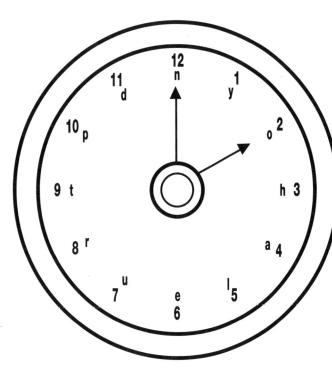

The Lord had
9 3 6   5 2 8 11   3 4 11

said to Abram,
4 11   9 2   4 8 4

"Leave your
5 6 4 6   1 2 7 8

country, your
2 7 12 9 8 1   1 2 7 8

people and
10 6 2 10 5 6   4 12 11

your father's
1 2 7 8   4 9 3 6 8

household and go to the
3 2 7 6 3 2 5 11   4 12 11   2   9 2   9 3 6

land I will show you." So Abram
5 4 12 11   5 5   3 2   1 2 7   2   4 8 4

left...Abram was seventy-five years
5 6 9   4 8 4   4   6 6 12 9 1   6   1 6 4 8

old. – Genesis 12:1,4
2 5 11

Challenge:

How can I follow Christ's call?
3 2   4 12   2 5 5 2   3 8 9   4 5 5

Wicked Cities
Genesis 14:12-13; 19:1-29

Lot was Abram's relative and traveled with him. When Lot and Abram parted ways, Lot settled and became wealthy in a city that was very sinful. God destroyed this city and another city. Lot and his family were saved. But Lot's wife looked back at the city as she was leaving, even though angels had instructed her not to do so. For her disobedience, Lot's wife was turned into a pillar of salt. Use the code below to find Lot's connection to Abram and the names of the two cities destroyed because of the people's wickedness.

1	2	3	4	5	6	7	8	9
P	N	W	C	R	A	H	O	E

10	11	12	13	14	15	16	17	18
B	S	D	G	T	F	I	M	K

,
___ ___   ___ ___ ___ ...___ ___ ___ ___ ___ ___
7 9   3 6 11   6 10 5 6 17 11

___ ___ ___ ___ ___ ___. ___ ___ ___   ___ ___ ___ ___ ___
2 9 1 7 9 3   14 7 9   14 8 3 2 11

___ ___   ___ ___ ___ ___ ___ ___ ___ ___ ___...
8 15   3 16 4 18 9 12 2 9 11 11

___ ___ ___ ___ ___   ___ ___ ___   ___ ___ ___ ___ ___ ___ ___ ___.
11 8 12 8 17   6 2 12   13 8 17 8 5 5 6 7

Wicked Cities

Answer

1	2	3	4	5	6	7	8	9
P	N	W	C	R	A	H	O	E

10	11	12	13	14	15	16	17	18
B	S	D	G	T	F	I	M	K

H e   w a s…A b r a m's
7 9   3 6 11   6 10 5 6 17 11

n e p h e w.   T h e   t o w n s
2 9 1 7 9 3   14 7 9   14 8 3 2 11

o f   w i c k e d n e s s…
8 15   3 16 4 18 9 12 2 8 11 11

S o d o m   a n d   G o m o r r a h.
11 8 12 8 17   6 2 12   13 8 17 8 5 5 6 7

A Child in Old Age

Genesis 18:1-15; 21:1-7

Sarah was 90 years old when she discovered she was going to have a child. She laughed at the very thought of becoming a mother at her age! The Lord asked Abraham why Sarah laughed and then asked him a question we can learn from even today. Use the bubble code to find the question from God and Sarah's response to the miracle birth of Isaac.

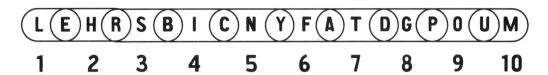

L (E) H (R) S (B) I (C) N (Y) F (A) T (D) G (P) O (U) M

1   2   3   4   5   6   7   8   9   10

Example: 6/7 = A (A is found in part of bubble 6 and bubble 7.)

___ ___ ___ ___ ___ ___ ___ ___ ___ ___ ___ ___ ___
 4   3   6/7 5 5/6 7   2   4   5   8   7   9   9

___ ___ ___ ___ ___ ___ ___ ___ ___ ___ ___ ___ ___ ___?
 2 6/7 2/3 7/8   6   9 2/3   7   2 1/2   1   9 2/3 7/8

- Genesis 18:14

___ ___ ___ ___ ___ ___ ___ ___ ___ ___ ___ ___ ___
 8   9 7/8   2 6/7 3   3/4 2/3 9 9/10 8   2   7

___ ___
10 1/2

___ ___ ___ ___ ___ ___ ___ ___.
 1 6/7 9/10 8   2   7 1/2 2/3

- Genesis 21:6

A Child in Old Age

Answer

L (E) H (R) S (B) I (C) N (Y) F (A) T (D) G (P) O (U) M

1   2   3   4   5   6   7   8   9   10

I s   a n y t h i n g   t o o
4 3   6/7 5 5/6 7 2 4 5 8   7 9 9

h a r d   f o r   t h e   L o r d?
2 6/7 2/3 7/8   6 9 2/3   7 2 1/2   1 9 2/3 7/8

- Genesis 18:14

G o d   h a s   b r o u g h t
8 9 7/8   2 6/7 3   3/4 2/3 9 9/10 8 2 7

m e   l a u g h t e r.   **- Genesis 21:6**
10 1/2   1 6/7 9/10 8 2   7 1/2 2/3

A Mighty Test
Genesis 22:1-14

God tested Abraham by asking him to do something incredible. Isaac was part of this test. Fill in the blanks with the numbered words to reveal what God asked Abraham to do. Then write the letters with asterisks (*) in the bottom blanks with matching numbers to find what Isaac learned from this test.

1. there	2. bound	3. Isaac	4. knife	5. and	6. altar
7. Abraham	8. son	9. arranged	10. reached	11. his	12. wood
13. the	14. out	15. He/he	16. laid	17. hand	18. slay
19. on	20. top	21. built	22. him	23. to	24. it
25. took	26. Then	27. an	28. of		

___ ___ ___ ___ ___
7 *2 21 27 6

___ ___ ___ ___
1 5 9 *9 13

___ ___ ___ ___. ___ ___
12 19 24 15 2 *7 11

___ ___ ___ ___ ___ ___
*11 8 *3 3 5 16 22

___ ___ ___, ___ ___ ___
19 13 6 *4 19 20 28 *6

___ ___ ___. ___ ___ ___
13 12 26 15

___ ___ ___ ___ ___
*10 10 14 11 *5 17 5

___ ___ ___ ___ ___
25 13 4 *1 23 *8 18

___ ___ ___. – Genesis 22:9b-10
11 *12 8

___ ___ ___ ___ ___ ___ ___ ___ ___ ___ ___ ___
1   2   3   4   5   6   7   8   9   10   11   12

21

A Mighty Test

Answer

1. there   2. bound   3. Isaac   4. knife   5. and   6. altar

7. Abraham   8. son   9. arranged   10. reached   11. his   12. wood

13. the   14. out   15. He/he   16. laid   17. hand   18. slay

19. on   20. top   21. built   22. him   23. to   24. it

25. took   26. Then   27. an   28. of

A b r a h a m   b u i l t   a n   a l t a r
7   *2   21   27   6

t h e r e   a n d   a r r a n g e d   t h e
1   5   9 *9   13

w o o d   o n   i t.   H e   b o u n d   h i s
12   19   24   15   2 *7   11

s o n   I s a a c   a n d   l a i d   h i m
*11 8   *3 3   5   16   22

o n   t h e   a l t a r,   o n   t o p   o f
19   13   6 *4   19   20   28 *6

t h e   w o o d.   T h e n   h e
13   12   26   15

r e a c h e d   o u t   h i s   h a n d   a n d
*10 10   14   11   *5 17   5

t o o k   t h e   k n i f e   t o   s l a y
25   13   4 *1   23   *8 18

h i s   s o n.   – Genesis 22:9b-10 (Note: God stopped Abraham. Isaac was unhurt.)
11   *12 8

F a i t h f u l n e s s
1   2   3   4   5   6   7   8   9   10   11   12

Twin Trickery
Genesis 25:24-25; 27:1-40

Jacob tricked his twin brother, Esau, into selling the family birthright for a bowl of stew. Then Jacob tricked Isaac, their father, into thinking that Jacob was Esau, thereby stealing Esau's blessing. Use the oven dial code to find what Esau's birthright and blessing included.

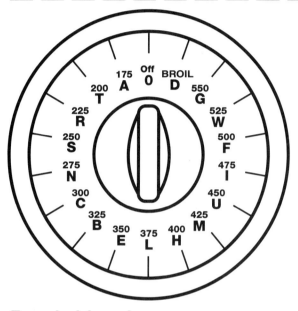

Esau's birthright:

___ ___ ___   ___ ___ ___ ___ ___ -
200 400 350   500 475 225 250 200

,

___ ___ ___ ___ ___
325 OFF 225 275 250

___ P ___ ___ ___ ___ ___ ___
250   350 300 475 175 375

___ ___ ___ ___ ___ ___ -
475 275 400 350 225 475

___ ___ ___ ___ ___
200 175 275 300 350

Esau's blessings:

___ ___ ___   ___ ___ ___ ___ ___ ___   ___ ___ ___ ___ ___ ___ ___ ___;
200 400 350   350 175 225 200 400 250   225 475 300 400 275 350 250 250

___ ___ ___ ___ ___ ___ ___ ___ ___   ___ ___   ___ ___ ___ ___ ___
175 325 450 275 BROIL 175 275 300 350 OFF 500   550 225 175 475 275

___ ___ ___   ___ ___ ___ ___ ___; ___ P___ ___ ___ ___ ___ ___   ___ ___ ___ ___
175 275 BROIL 525 475 275 350 175   225 OFF 425 475 250 350   200 400 175 200

___ ___ ___ ___ ___ ___ ___   ___ ___ ___ ___ ___ BROIL   ___ ___ ___ V___   ___ ___ ___
275 175 200 475 OFF 275 250   525 OFF 450 375 BROIL   250 350 225 350   400 475 425

___ ___   ___ ___ ___ ___ ___ BROIL   ___ ___   ___ ___ ___ ___ BROIL   ___ V___ ___
400 350   525 OFF 450 375 BROIL   325 350   375 OFF 225 BROIL   OFF 350 225

___ ___ ___   ___ ___ ___ ___ ___ ___ ___ ___; ___   ___ ___ ___ ___ ___ ___   ___ ___
400 475 250   325 225 OFF 200 400 350 225 250   175   300 450 225 250 350   200 OFF

___ ___ ___ ___ ___   ___ ___ ___   ___ ___ ___ ___ ___   ___ ___ ___;
200 400 OFF 250 350   525 400 OFF   300 450 225 250 350   400 475 425

___ ___ ___ ___ ___ ___ ___ ___ ___   ___ ___   ___ ___ ___ ___ ___ ___
325 375 350 250 250 475 275 550 250   200 OFF   200 400 OFF 250 350

___ ___ ___   ___ ___ ___ ___ ___   ___ ___ ___.   (from Genesis 25:24-34; 27:27-39)
525 400 OFF   325 375 350 250 250   400 475 425

23

Twin Trickery

Answer

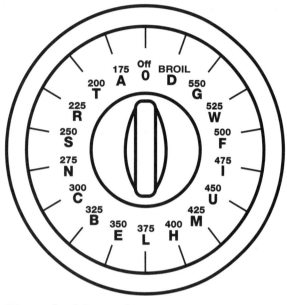

Esau's birthright:

T h e   f i r s t-
200 400 350   500 475 225 250 200

b o r n ' s
325 OFF 225 275 250

s P e c i a l
250 350 300 475 175 375

i n h e r i-
475 275 400 350 225 475

t a n c e
200 175 275 300 350

Esau's blessings:

T h e   e a r t h ' s   r i c h n e s s;
200 400 350   350 175 225 200 400 250   225 475 300 400 275 350 250 250

a b u n d a n c e   o f   g r a i n
175 325 450 275 BROIL 175 275 300 350   OFF 500   550 225 175 475 275

a n d   w i n e;   a   P r o m i s e   t h a t
175 275 BROIL   525 475 275 350   175   225 OFF 425 475 250 350   200 400 175 200

n a t i o n s   w o u l d   s e r V e   h i m
275 175 200 475 OFF 275 250   525 OFF 450 375 BROIL   250 350 225 350   400 475 425

h e   w o u l d   b e   l o r d   o V e r
400 350   525 OFF 450 375 BROIL   325 350   375 OFF 225 BROIL   OFF 350 225

h i s   b r o t h e r s;   a   c u r s e   t o
400 475 250   325 225 OFF 200 400 350 225 250   175   300 450 225 250 350   200 OFF

t h o s e   w h o   c u r s e   h i m;
200 400 OFF 250 350   525 400 OFF   300 450 225 250 350   400 475 425

b l e s s i n g s   t o   t h o s e
325 375 350 250 250 475 275 550 250   200 OFF   200 400 OFF 250 350

w h o   b l e s s   h i m. (from Genesis 25:24-34; 27:27-39)
525 400 OFF   325 375 350 250 250   400 475 425

24

Struggling to Overcome
Genesis 32:22-32

Jacob had a difficult life. When he was young, he struggled against his twin brother, Esau. Later, he struggled with Laban, Rachel's father, to win Rachel as his wife. He even wrestled with an angel of God. During the fight with the angel, God changed Jacob's name. First, find what God would call Jacob. Second, find why Jacob got this name. Use the letters on the left (L) and right (R) sides of the ladder to fill in the blanks. (Count the rungs from the bottom up.)

Example: L6 = E (Left side, 6th rung)

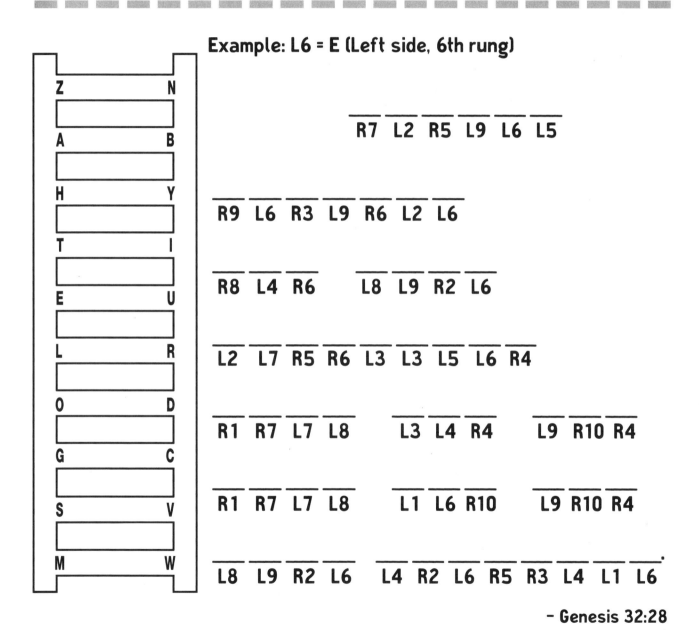

— Genesis 32:28

Struggling to Overcome

Answer

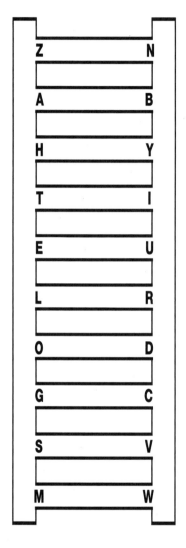

I s r a e l
R7 L2 R5 L9 L6 L5

B e c a u s e
R9 L6 R3 L9 R6 L2 L6

y o u   h a v e
R8 L4 R6   L8 L9 R2 L6

s t r u g g l e d
L2 L7 R5 R6 L3 L3 L5 L6 R4

w i t h   G o d   a n d
R1 R7 L7 L8   L3 L4 R4   L9 R10 R4

w i t h   m e n   a n d
R1 R7 L7 L8   L1 L6 R10   L9 R10 R4

h a v e   o v e r c o m e.
L8 L9 R2 L6   L4 R2 L6 R5 R3 L4 L1 L6

– Genesis 32:28

A Special Brother
Genesis 26:16-20; 43:26-31

Benjamin was the youngest of 12 brothers. He was extra special to his brothers and to his father. The names of all the brothers are below. Use the letters in their names to find out (1) What made Benjamin special to his father, Jacob, and (2) what made Benjamin special to his brother Joseph?

1	2	3	4	5	6	7	8	9	10	11	12
R	S	L	J	I	Z	J	B	D	N	G	A
E	I	E	U	S	E	O	E	A	A	A	S
U	M	V	D	S	B	S	N	N	P	D	H
B	E	I	A	A	U	E	J		H		E
E	O		H	C	L	P	A		T		R
N	N			H	U	H	M		A		
				A	N		I		L		
				R			N				
							I				

Example: 5
3
= S (5th name/3rd letter)

What made Benjamin special to his father, Jacob?

8	9	5	7	1	5		6	7	3	2	3	8	11		5	11	5	7	1	10
4	2	5	2	4	3		3	4	1	5	3	2	3		8	2	5	6	5	7

4	8	1	9		11	3	3	2	6	11		1	5	1	10	12		10	7
3	7	2	1		1	4	3	2	7	1		4	1	1	5	3		5	2

(from Genesis 35:18-20)

6	3	10	7	5	2	10	1
3	2	1	1	7	3	8	6

What made Benjamin special to Joseph?

10	3	W	5	7		4	2	12	12	10	4	5		7	1	6	Y
4	2		4	3		1	5	2	4	3	5	2		2	6	5	

F

4	10	3		1	12	2	10	5	2	5
2	7	1		4	5	5	5	6	4	8

(from Genesis 43:29)

A Special Brother

Answer

1	2	3	4	5	6	7	8	9	10	11	12
R	S	L	J	I	Z	J	B	D	N	G	A
E	I	E	U	S	E	O	E	A	A	A	S
U	M	V	D	S	B	S	N	N	P	D	H
B	E	I	A	A	U	E	J		H		E
E	O		H	C	L	P	A		T		R
N	N			H	U	H	M		A		
				A	N		I		L		
				R			N				
							I				

What made Benjamin special to his father, Jacob?

J a c o b's   b e l o v e d   R a c h e l
8 9 5 7 1 5   6 7 3 2 3 8 11   5 11 5 7 1 10
4 2 5 2 4 3   3 4 1 5 3 2 3   8 2 5 6 5 7

d i e d   g i v i n g   b i r t h   t o
4 8 1 9   11 3 3 2 6 11   1 5 1 10 12   10 7
3 7 2 1   1 4 3 2 7 1   4 1 1 5 3   5 2

B e n j a m i n, (from Genesis 35:18-20)
6 3 10 7 5 2 10 1
3 2 1 1 7 3 8 6

What made Benjamin special to Joseph?

H e   w a s   J o s e p h's   o n l y
10 3   5 7   4 2 12 12 10 4 5   7 1 6
4 2   4 3   1 5 2 4 3 5 2   2 6 5

F u l l   b r o t h e r. (from Genesis 43:29)
4 10 3   1 12 2 10 5 2 5
2 7 1   4 5 5 5 6 4 8

28

In a Special Place
Matthew 1:17

Tamar had been married to Judah's son Er (Genesis 38:6). Er was a wicked man who died. He had no children. Through a series of circumstances, Judah became the father of Tamar's twin sons, Perez and Zerah. Perez was in the direct line of ancestry for David and Jesus. Because of this, Tamar's name is listed in Matthew 1. In the puzzle, decide which word in each set doesn't belong. Write the first letter of that word on the line below it to reveal where Tamar's name appears.

tree	emblem	stool	rug	sister
jug	pencil	hat	umbrella	dress
leaf	paper	glove	carpet	pants,
____	____	____	____	____

gum	rocker	flower	car	apple
radio	envelope	nose	truck	sock
stereo	chair	plant	egg	shoe
____	____	____	____	____ -

baby	organ	red	computer
lollipop	peas	blue	yoyo
crawl	carrots	grass	printer
____	____	____	____

In a Special Place

Answer

tree	emblem	stool	rug	sister
jug	pencil	hat	umbrella	dress
leaf	paper	glove	carpet	pants,
__J__	__e__	__s__	__u__	__s__ '

gum	rocker	flower	car	apple
radio	envelope	nose	truck	sock
stereo	chair	plant	egg	shoe
__g__	__e__	__n__	__e__	__a__ -

baby	organ	red	computer
lollipop	peas	blue	yoyo
crawl	carrots	grass	printer
__l__	__o__	__g__	__y__

The Song of Miriam
Exodus 15:19-21

Miriam was Aaron and Moses' sister. She sang a song of great joy after the Israelites crossed the Red Sea. Use the musical notes to fill in the spaces to reveal her song. Continue at the bottom to find the instrument she used and what else she and the other women did to show praise.

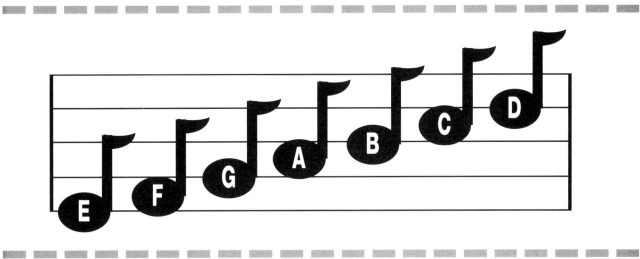

"Sin__ to th__ Lor__, __or h__ is

hi__hly __x__lt__ __. Th__ hors__ __n__

its ri__ __r h__ h__s hurl__ __ into

th__ s__ __." – **Exodus 15:21**

T__m__ourin__

__ __n__in__

31

The Song of Miriam

Answer

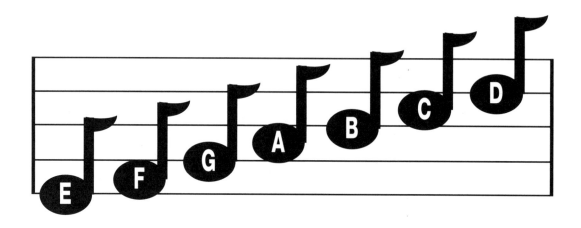

"Si ng to the Lor d, for he is highly exalted. The horse and its rider he has hurled into the sea." – Exodus 15:21

Tambourine

Dancing

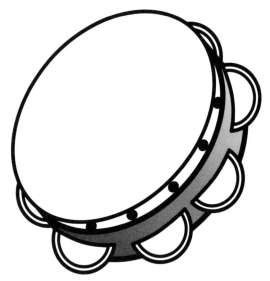

The Tablets of Law
Exodus 20:1-17

God loved Moses. Moses kept God's laws, led the people out of Egypt, performed miracles, called down plagues and did much more. At Mt. Sinai, God gave Moses stone tablets with special laws on them. Moses was angered when he came down because the people were worshiping an idol. He threw down the tablets and broke them. God wrote a second set so the people would know His laws. Use the radio dial to reveal some of what God wrote on these tablets for Moses and all people.

```
FM 88 O   92 I   96 N   100 H   104 R   106 U   108 L
AM 540 G   650 A   800 M   1000 T   1300 Y   1400 E   1600 S
```

(1) (2) (3) (4)
(5) (6) (7) (8)

1. __ __ __
AM1300 FM88 FM106

__ __ __ __ __
AM1600 FM100 AM650 FM108 FM108

__ __ V __
FM100 AM650   AM1400

__ __
FM96 FM88

__ __ __ __ __
FM88 AM1000 FM100 AM1400 FM104

__ __ D __   B __ F __ __ __   __ __.
AM540 FM88 AM1600 AM1400 FM88 FM104 AM1400 AM800 AM1400

2. __ __ __   __ __ __ __ __   __ __ __
AM1300 FM88 FM106   AM1600 FM100 AM650 FM108 FM108   FM96 FM88 AM1000

__ __ K __   __ __ W__ __ __ __ __ P
AM800 AM650 AM1400   FM88 FM104   FM88 FM104 AM1600 FM100 FM92

__ __ __   __ D __ __ __ __.
AM650 FM96 AM1300   FM92 FM88 FM108 AM1600

3. D __   __ __ __   __ __ __   __ __ __
FM88   FM96 FM88 AM1000   FM106 AM1600 AM1400   AM1000 FM100 AM1400

__ __ __ D' __   __ __ __ __   __ __
FM108 FM88 FM104 AM1600 FM96 AM650 AM800 AM1400 FM92 FM96

V __ __ __.   (from Exodus 20)
AM650 FM92 FM96

33

The Tablets of Law

Answer

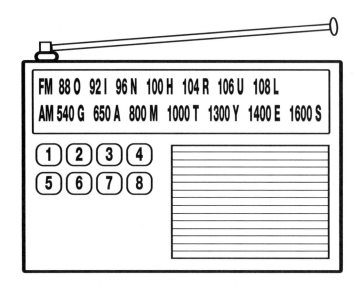

FM 88 O 92 I 96 N 100 H 104 R 106 U 108 L
AM 540 G 650 A 800 M 1000 T 1300 Y 1400 E 1600 S

1 2 3 4
5 6 7 8

1. Y o u
AM1300 FM88 FM106

s h a l l
AM1600 FM100 AM650 FM108 FM108

h a v e
FM100 AM650   AM1400

n o
FM96 FM88

o t h e r
FM88 AM1000 FM100 AM1400 FM104

g o D s B e F o r e   m e.
AM540 FM88 AM1600 AM1400 FM88 FM104 AM1400 AM800 AM1400

2. Y o u   s h a l l   n o t
AM1300 FM88 FM106 AM1600 FM100 AM650 FM108 FM108 FM96 FM88 AM1000

m a K e   o r W o r s h i P
AM800 AM650 AM1400 FM88 FM104 FM88 FM104 AM1600 FM100 FM92

a n y   i D o l s.
AM650 FM96 AM1300 FM92 FM88 FM108 AM1600

3. D o   n o t   u s e   t h e
   FM88 FM96 FM88 AM1000 FM106 AM1600 AM1400 AM1000 FM100 AM1400

L o r D' s   n a m e   i n
FM108 FM88 FM104 AM1600 FM96 AM650 AM800 AM1400 FM92 FM96

V a i n. (from Exodus 20)
AM650 FM92 FM96

34

And the Walls Came Tumbling Down
Joshua 6:1-21

God told Joshua He would deliver Jericho into his hands. Write down the days of the week, with Sunday as the first day. Use the first letter of the first day, the second letter of the second day, third letter of the third day, etc., except on Day Five. On Day Five use letter number six. Write these letters in the blank spaces to learn of God's unusual and specific directions to Joshua so that the city of Jericho would fall.

Day one: _____ __   Day two: _____ __

Day three: _____ __   Day four: _____ __

Day five: _____ __   Day six: _____ __

Day seven: _____ __

"M_rch   _r_u_ _   th_   cit_   _ _c_   with   _ll   th_

_rm_ _   m_ _.   _ _   _hi_   f_r   _ix   _ _ _ _.   H_v_

_ _v_ _   pri_ _t_   c_rr_   trump_t_   _f   r_m_'   h_r_ _

i_   fr_ _t   _f   th_   _rk.   _ _   th_   _ _v_ _th   _ _ _,

m_rch   _r_u_ _   th_   cit_   _ _v_ _   tim_ _,   with   th_

pri_ _t_   bl_wi_g   th_   trump_t_.   Wh_ _ _   _ _u   h_ _r

th_m   _ _u_ _   _   l_ _g   bl_ _t   _ _   th_   trump_t_,

h_v_   _ll   th_   p_ _pl_   giv_   _   l_u_   _h_ut;   th_ _ _

th_   w_ll   _f   th_   cit_   will   _ _ll_p_ _   _ _ _ _   th_

p_ _pl_   will   g_   up,   _v_r_   m_ _   _tr_ight   i_."

– Joshua 6:3-5

35

And the Walls Came Tumbling Down

Answer

Day one: <u>Sunday</u> <u>S</u>   **Day two:** <u>Monday</u> <u>O</u>

Day three: <u>Tuesday</u> <u>E</u>   **Day four:** <u>Wednesday</u> <u>N</u>

Day five: <u>Thursday</u> <u>D</u>   **Day six:** <u>Friday</u>   <u>Y</u>

Day seven: <u>Saturday</u> <u>A</u>

"March around the city once with all the armed men. Do this for six days. Have seven priests carry trumpets of rams' horns in front of the ark. On the seventh day, march around the city seven times, with the priests blowing the trumpets. When you hear them sound a long blast on the trumpets, have all the people give a loud shout; then the wall of the city will collapse and the people will go up, every man straight in."

– Joshua 6:3-5

A Test for God, a Test for Gideon
Judges 6

God instructed Gideon to raise an army against the Midianites. But Gideon lacked confidence, so he asked God for a sign of victory – not once but twice! God honored Gideon's requests but then tested Gideon to see if he had the faith it took to be victorious. Find Gideon's requests of God. Fill in the blanks with every other vowel, beginning with "I," to read Gideon's first request. Then below that read what he requested from God next.

I A E E O I A O I U O A O E I I O O U U I Y A A E E I I A O E U Y Y Y A A E A I O O U
U A Y E A O E I I E O O U O Y I A I E A I E O A U O Y O A E E E I E O O U E Y E A I
E O I O O I U E Y E A I E E I O O Y U O Y E A E E E I E O A U A Y E A O E U I I O Y
U E A I E I I O O A U O Y U A I E A I E O I U A Y E A Y E Y I A O A U O Y U A A E I I
A O A U I Y A A A O E I E O I U E Y O A O E E I E O A U Y Y E A E E A I Y O E O U U
E Y E A E E E I E O E U E Y A A U E O I U O E U E Y A A O E U I O O A U E Y

G_d__n s__d t_ G_d, "_f y__ w_ll s_v_ _sr__l

b_ m_ h_nd _s y__ h_v_ pr_m_s_d - l__k, _ w_ll

pl_c_ _ w__l fl__c_ _n th_ thr_sh_ng fl__r.

_f th_r_ _s d_w _nl_ _n th_ fl__c_ _nd _ll

th_ gr__nd _s dr_, th_n _ w_ll kn_w th_t y__

w_ll s_v_ _sr__l b_ m_ h_nd, _s y__ s__d."

_nd th_t _s wh_t h_pp_n_d. G_d__n r_s_ __rl_

th_ n_xt d__; h_ sq___z_d th_ fl__c_ _nd

wr_ng __t th_ d_w - _ b_wlf_l _f w_t_r.

Then Gideon said to God, "Do not be angry with me. Let me make just one more request. Allow me one more test with the fleece. This time make the fleece dry and the ground covered with dew." That night God did so. Only the fleece was dry; all the ground was covered with dew. - Judges 6:36-40

A Test for God, a Test for Gideon

Answer

IAEEOIAOIUOAOEIIOOUUIYAAEEIIAOEUYYYAAEAIOOU
UAYEAOEIIEOOUOYIAIEAIEOAUOYOAEEEIEOOUEYEAI
EOIOOIUEYEAIEEIOOYUOYEAEEEIEOAUAYEAOEUIIOY
UEAIEIIOOAUOYUAIEAIEOIUAYEAYEYIAOAUOYUAAEII
AOAUIYAAAOEIEOIUEYOAOEEIEOAUYYEAEEAIYOEOUU
EYEAEEEIEOEUEYAAUEOIUOEUEYAAOEUIOOAUEY

Gideon said to God, "If you will save Isreal
by my hand as you have promised - look, I will
place a wool fleece on the threshing floor.
If there is dew only on the fleece and all
the ground is dry, then I will know that you
will save Israel by my hand, as you said."
And that is what happened. Gideon rose early
the next day; he squeezed the fleece and
wrung out the dew - a bowlful of water.

Eli's Instructions
1 Samuel 3:1-19

When God gave Hannah a son, she vowed to give him back to God. She kept her promise by taking young Samuel to the temple and allowing the priest, Eli, to raise him. One night Samuel heard a voice. He thought Eli was calling him. Then Eli realized it was actually the Lord speaking to Samuel! Use the telephone dial to find what Eli told Samuel to do.

Example: 3.1 = D; 3rd number, 1st one in set

4.1 6.3   2.1 6.2 3.1   5.3 4.3 3.2

" _____   _____   _____

3.1 6.3 9.1 6.2   2.1 6.2 3.1   4.3 3.3

_____,   _____   _____

4.2 3.2   2.3 2.1 5.3 5.3 7.4   9.3 6.3 8.2

_____   _____   _____,

7.4 2.1 9.3   7.4 7.1 3.2 2.1 5.2   5.3 6.3 7.3 3.1

_____,   ' _____,   _____,

3.3 6.3 7.3   9.3 6.3 8.2 7.3

_____   _____

7.4 3.2 7.3 8.3 2.1 6.2 8.1   4.3 7.4

_____   _____

5.3 4.3 7.4 8.1 3.2 6.2 4.3 6.2 4.1

_____.' "

— 1 Samuel 3:9

39

Eli's Instructions

Answer

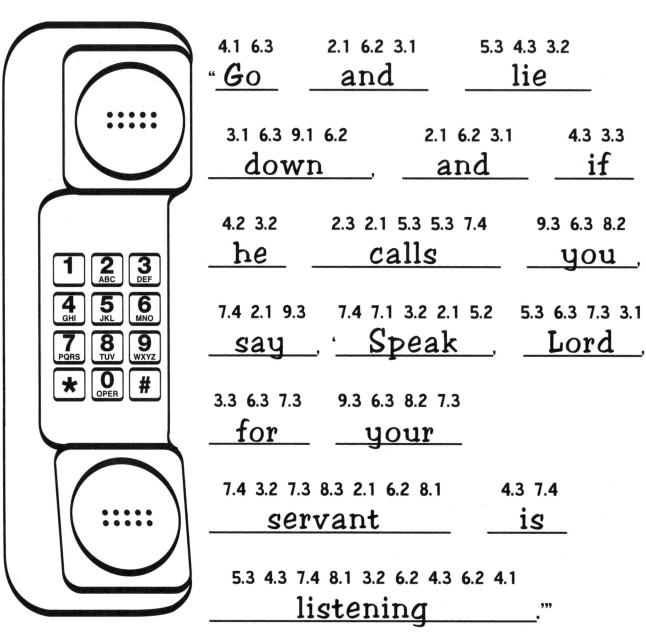

4.1 6.3　　2.1 6.2 3.1　　5.3 4.3 3.2
"__Go__　__and__　__lie__

3.1 6.3 9.1 6.2　　2.1 6.2 3.1　　4.3 3.3
__down__,　__and__　__if__

4.2 3.2　　2.3 2.1 5.3 5.3 7.4　　9.3 6.3 8.2
__he__　__calls__　__you__,

7.4 2.1 9.3　　7.4 7.1 3.2 2.1 5.2　　5.3 6.3 7.3 3.1
__say__, '__Speak__,　__Lord__,

3.3 6.3 7.3　　9.3 6.3 8.2 7.3
__for__　__your__

7.4 3.2 7.3 8.3 2.1 6.2 8.1　　4.3 7.4
__servant__　__is__

5.3 4.3 7.4 8.1 3.2 6.2 4.3 6.2 4.1
__listening__.'"

– 1 Samuel 3:9

40

A Special Anointing
1 Samuel 16:1-13

Samuel was given a special commission. He was instructed to anoint the next king of Israel. The young man God selected seemed an unlikely choice. Use the horn cup measurements to reveal the story.

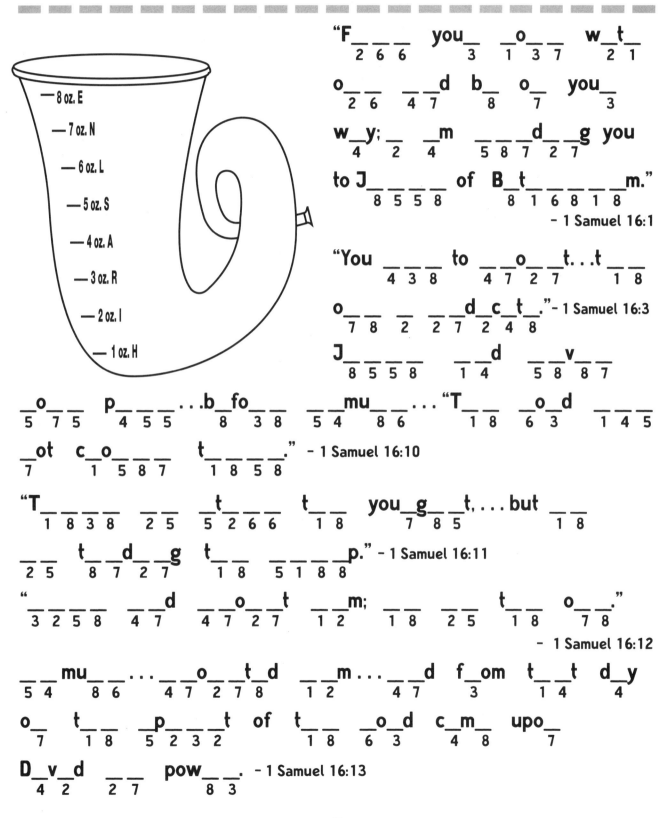

—8 oz. E
—7 oz. N
—6 oz. L
—5 oz. S
—4 oz. A
—3 oz. R
—2 oz. I
—1 oz. H

"F_ _ _   you_ _o_ _ w_t_
  2 6 6   3   1 3 7   2 1

o_ _   _d b_ o_ you_
 2 6   4 7   8   7   3

w_y; _ _m _ _ _d_ _g you
 4   2 4   5 8 7 2 7

to J_ _ _ _ of B_t_ _ _ _ _m."
    8 5 5 8   8 1 6 8 1 8
                      - 1 Samuel 16:1

"You _ _ _ to _ _o_ _t...t _ _
       4 3 8   4 7 2 7   1 8

o_ _ _ _ _ _d_c_t_."- 1 Samuel 16:3
 7 8 2 2 7 2 4 8

J_ _ _ _   _d   _ _v_ _
 8 5 5 8   1 4   5 8 8 7

_o_ _ p_ _ _...b_fo_ _ _ _mu_ _... "T_ _ _o_d   _ _ _
5 7 5 4 5 5   8 3 8   5 4 8 6   1 8 6 3   1 4 5

_ot c_o_ _ _ t_ _ _ _." - 1 Samuel 16:10
7   1 5 8 7   1 8 5 8

"T_ _ _ _ _ _ _t_ _ _ t_ _ you_g_ _t,...but _ _
   1 8 3 8   2 5 5 2 6 6 1 8   7 8 5   1 8

_ _ t_ _d_ _g t_ _ _ _ _ _p." - 1 Samuel 16:11
2 5 8 7 2 7   1 8 5 1 8 8

"_ _ _ _ _d _ _o_ _t _ _m; _ _ _ _ t_ _ o_ _."
 3 2 5 8 4 7 4 7 2 7 1 2   1 8 2 5 1 8   7 8
                                        - 1 Samuel 16:12

_ _mu_... _ _o_ _t_d _ _m... _ _d f_om t_ _t d_y
5 4 8 6   4 7 2 7 8   1 2   4 7   3   1 4   4

o_ t_ _ _ _p_ _ _t of t_ _ _o_d c_m_ upo_
 7 1 8   5 2 3 2   1 8 6 3   4 8   7

D_v_d _ _ pow_ _. - 1 Samuel 16:13
4 2   2 7 8 3

A Special Anointing

Answer

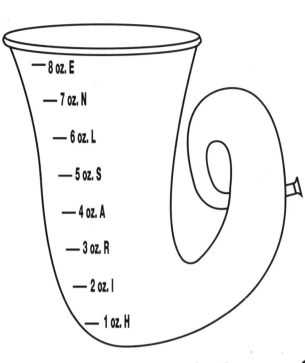

8 oz. E
7 oz. N
6 oz. L
5 oz. S
4 oz. A
3 oz. R
2 oz. I
1 oz. H

"Fill your horn with
2 6 6   3   1 3 7   2 1

oil and be on your
2 6   4 7   8   7   3

way; I am sending you
4   2   4   5 8 7 2 7

to Jesse of Bethlehem."
8 5 5 8   8 1 6 8 1 8

– 1 Samuel 16:1

"You are to anoint...the
4 3 8   4 7 2 7   1 8

one I indicate."– 1 Samuel 16:3
7 8   2   2 7 2 4 8

Jesse   had   seven
8 5 5 8   1 4   5 8 8 7

sons pass...before Samuel..."The Lord has
5 7 5   4 5 5   8 3 8   5 4 8 6   1 8   6 3   1 4 5

not chosen these." – 1 Samuel 16:10
7   1 5 8 7   1 8 5 8

"There is still the youngest,...but he
1 8 3 8   2 5   5 2 6 6   1 8   7 8 5   1 8

is tending the sheep." – 1 Samuel 16:11
2 5   8 7 2 7   1 8   5 1 8 8

"Rise and anoint him; he is the one."
3 2 5 8   4 7   4 7 2 7   1 2   1 8   2 5   1 8   7 8

– 1 Samuel 16:12

Samuel...anointed him...and from that day
5 4   8 6   4 7 2 7 8   1 2   4 7   3   1 4   4

on the spirit of the Lord came upon
7   1 8   5 2 3 2   1 8   6 3   4 8   7

David in power. – 1 Samuel 16:13
4 2   2 7   8 3

42

Abigail's Gift
1 Samuel 25:1-35

Abigail was intelligent and beautiful. Her husband, Nabal, is described in the Bible as surly and mean. David and his men needed food. They requested some from Nabal. He refused to help them despite the protection David and his soldiers had given him and his property. When Abigail heard, she took matters into her own hands. Compute each problem to find how much she sent David of each item, then use the clues to figure out the items.

800 x 3 ÷ 4 - 500 + 100 = _____

loaves of _____

(baked in a loaf pan, made of grain, often used for sandwiches)

96 ÷ 3 x 6 + 8 - 198 = _____

skins of _____

(fermented grape juice, packaged in bottles, in Bible days often used as the beverage instead of water)

495 + 55 ÷ 11 x 2 - 95 = _____

dressed _____

(fuzzy animals, fur is wool, say "Baa")

835 x 4 ÷ 5 + 32 - 305 ÷ 5 +1 - 60 ÷ 4 = _____

seahs (about a bushel) of roasted _____

(wheat, oats, barley, rye, corn)

1600 - 511 + 51 ÷ 2 - 470 = _____

cakes of _____

(begin as grapes, dried and become a nutritious snack)

660 + 45 x 3 + 5 ÷ 2 + 40 - 100 ÷ 5 = _____

cakes of pressed _____

(oblong, pear-shaped fruit; type of "Newton")

(from 1 Samuel 25:3-19)

Abigail's Gift

Answer

800 x 3 ÷ 4 - 500 + 100 = <u>200</u>

loaves of <u>bread</u>

(baked in a loaf pan, made of grain, often used for sandwiches)

96 ÷ 3 x 6 + 8 - 198 = <u>2</u>

skins of <u>wine</u>

(fermented grape juice, packaged in bottles, in Bible days
often used as the beverage instead of water)

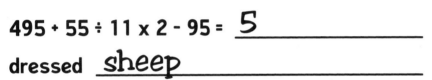

495 + 55 ÷ 11 x 2 - 95 = <u>5</u>

dressed <u>sheep</u>

(fuzzy animals, fur is wool, say "Baa")

835 x 4 ÷ 5 + 32 - 305 ÷ 5 +1 - 60 ÷ 4 = <u>5</u>

seahs (about a bushel) of roasted <u>grain</u>

(wheat, oats, barley, rye, corn)

1600 - 511 + 51 ÷ 2 - 470 = <u>100</u>

cakes of <u>raisins</u>

(begin as grapes, dried and become a nutritious snack)

660 + 45 x 3 + 5 ÷ 2 + 40 - 100 ÷ 5 = <u>200</u>

cakes of pressed <u>figs</u>

(oblong, pear-shaped fruit; type of "Newton")   (from 1 Samuel 25:3-19)

A Prayer of Thanksgiving
2 Samuel 2:1-10; Psalm 113; Luke 1:46-55

Hannah offered a prayer of thanksgiving when God answered her prayer for a child. This prayer is found in 1 Samuel 2:1-10. The psalmist, many years later, used part of Hannah's prayer in Psalm 113. Still later, Mary, the mother of Jesus, used some of the same words when she was thankful in Luke 1:46-55. Use the graph to find Hannah's prayer as written in Psalm 113.

	10	11	12	13	14	15	16	17
1	home	people	his	woman	glory	0	their	lifts
2	raises	as	our	look	enthroned	one	who	earth
3	poor	name	it	and	sets	her	now	of
4	forever-more	where	place	praise	rising	exalted	a	heavens
5	mother	the	settles	happy	barren	Lord	be	who
6	down	both	from	above	in	He	high	to
7	let	all	needy	servants	like	sun	heap	princes
8	seats	God	ash	stoops	them	dust	sits	with
9	nations	on		over		praised	is	children

_____ _____ _____. _____, _____ _____ _____ _____ _____,
4/13   5/11   5/15   4/13   1/15   7/13   3/17   5/11   5/15

_____ _____ _____ _____ _____ _____. _____ _____ _____
4/13   5/11   3/11   3/17   5/11   5/15   7/10   5/11   3/11

_____ _____ _____ _____ _____ _____ _____ _____ _____.
3/17   5/11   5/15   5/16   9/15   6/11   3/16   3/13   4/10

_____ _____ _____ _____ _____ _____ _____ _____ _____
6/12   5/11   4/14   3/17   5/11   7/15   6/17   5/11   4/12

_____ _____ _____ _____ _____ _____ _____ _____ _____
4/11   3/12   3/14   5/11   3/11   3/17   5/11   5/15   9/16

_____ _____ _____. _____ _____ _____ _____ _____ _____
6/17   5/16   9/15   5/11   5/15   9/16   4/15   9/13   7/11

_____ _____ _____, _____ _____ _____ _____ . . . . _____ _____ _____
5/11   9/10   1/12   1/14   6/13   5/11   4/17   6/15   5/12

_____ _____ _____ _____ _____ _____ _____ _____ _____
5/11   5/14   1/13   6/14   3/15   1/10   2/11   4/16   5/13

_____ _____ _____. _____ _____ _____.
5/10   3/17   9/17   4/13   5/11   5/15   **– Psalm 113**

A Prayer of Thanksgiving

Answer

1	home	people	his	woman	glory	0	their	lifts
2	raises	as	our	look	enthroned	one	who	earth
3	poor	name	it	and	sets	her	now	of
4	forever-more	where	place	praise	rising	exalted	a	heavens
5	mother	the	settles	happy	barren	Lord	be	who
6	down	both	from	above	in	He	high	to
7	let	all	needy	servants	like	sun	heap	princes
8	seats	God	ash	stoops	them	dust	sits	with
9	nations	on		over		praised	is	children
	10	**11**	**12**	**13**	**14**	**15**	**16**	**17**

Praise the Lord. Praise, O servants of the Lord,
4/13   5/11   5/15   4/13   1/15   7/13   3/17   5/11   5/15

praise the name of the Lord. Let the name
4/13   5/11   3/11   3/17   5/11   5/15   7/10   5/11   3/11

of the Lord be praised both now and forevermore.
3/17   5/11   5/15   5/16   9/15   6/11   3/16   3/13   4/10

From the rising of the sun to the place
6/12   5/11   4/14   3/17   5/11   7/15   6/17   5/11   4/12

where it sets the name of the Lord is
4/11   3/12   3/14   5/11   3/11   3/17   5/11   5/15   9/16

to be praised. The Lord is exalted over all
6/17   5/16   9/15   5/11   5/15   9/16   4/15   9/13   7/11

the nations, his glory above the heavens.... He settles
5/11   9/10   1/12   1/14   6/13   5/11   4/17   6/15   5/12

the barren woman in her home as a happy
5/11   5/14   1/13   6/14   3/15   1/10   2/11   4/16   5/13

mother of children. Praise the Lord.
5/10   3/17   9/17   4/13   5/11   5/15

— Psalm 113

46

The Time Will Come
Isaiah 7:13-14; Matthew 1:22-23

Biblical prophets predicted events that would happen in the future. The prophet Isaiah predicted the coming of Christ. Use the clock to reveal his prediction by writing the letter for each number under the line. Use the numbers above the letters to find out what "Immanuel" means.

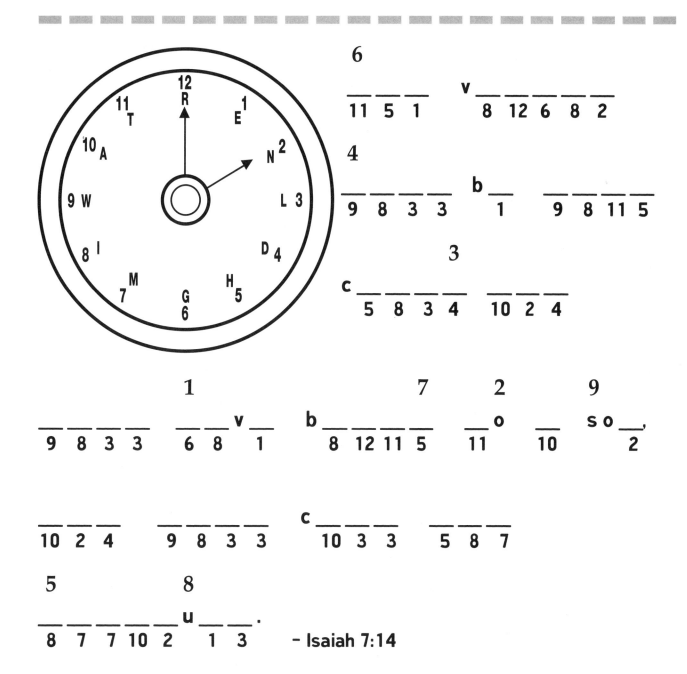

6
___ ___ ___ v ___ ___ ___ ___
11 5 1   8 12 6 8 2

4
___ ___ ___ ___ b ___ ___ ___ ___ ___
9 8 3 3   1   9 8 11 5

3
c ___ ___ ___ ___ ___ ___ ___
  5 8 3 4   10 2 4

1   7   2   9
___ ___ ___ ___ ___ ___ v ___ b ___ ___ ___ ___ ___ o ___ ___ s o ___,
9 8 3 3   6 8   1   8 12 11 5   11   10   2

___ ___ ___ ___ ___ ___ ___ c ___ ___ ___ ___ ___ ___
10 2 4   9 8 3 3   10 3 3   5 8 7

5   8
___ ___ ___ ___ ___ ___ u ___ ___ .
8 7 7 10 2   1 3   – Isaiah 7:14

What does Immanuel mean?

" ___ ___ ___ ___ ___ ___ ___ ___ ___ " (from Matthew 1:23)
  1 2 3   4 5 6 7   8 9

47

The Time Will Come

Answer

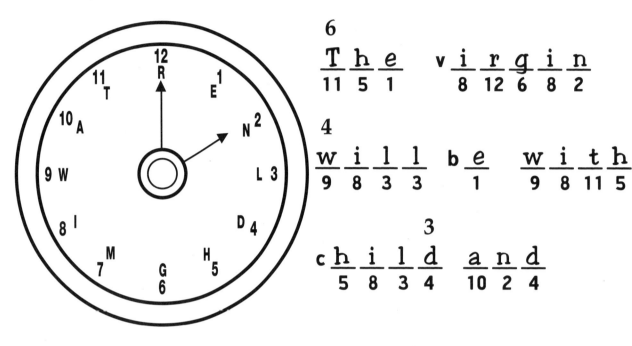

6
T h e   v i r g i n
11 5 1   8 12 6 8 2

4
w i l l   b e   w i t h
9 8 3 3   1   9 8 11 5

3
c h i l d   a n d
5 8 3 4   10 2 4

1   7   2   9
w i l l   g i v e   b i r t h   t o   a   s o n,
9 8 3 3   6 8 1   8 12 11 5   11   10   2

a n d   w i l l   c a l l   h i m
10 2 4   9 8 3 3   10 3 3   5 8 7

5   8
I m m a n u e l.
8 7 7 10 2 1 3   – Isaiah 7:14

What does Immanuel mean?

"G o d   w i t h   u s" (from Matthew 1:23)
1 2 3   4 5 6 7   8 9

48

Taking Time Backward
Isaiah 38:1-8

Hezekiah was a godly man and a good king. When Hezekiah became ill, the prophet Isaiah told him he would not recover from his illness. Hezekiah was sad and cried. He prayed to God about his sadness. Replace the given letter with the letter two places after it in the alphabet to find Hezekiah's prayer.

"PCKCKZCP, M JMPB, FMU G FYTC UYJICB ZCDMPC
  3   23   16   12   9

WMS DYGRFDSJJW YLB UGRF UFMJCFCYPRCB
     2   7   8   13   1

BCTMRGML YLB FYTC BMLC UFYR GQ EMMB
 21   4   10   20

GL WMSP CWCQ." (from Isaiah 38:3)
    15 6

God heard his prayer and added 15 years to his life, plus He delivered Hezekiah and the city from the king of Assyria. God gave a sign so Hezekiah would know He would do as He promised. Replace the letter given with the letter two places before it in the alphabet to find God's sign.

JG OCFG VJG UJCFQY QH VJG UWP IQ DCEM
24   18   26   5   19 22   11

VGP UVGRU QP VJG UWPFKCN. (from Isaiah 38:8)
25 17   14

What does this mean? Use the numbers in the prayer and sign to fill in the letters.

—— —— —— —— —— —— —— —— —— —— —— —— —— —— —— ——
 1   2   3   4   5   6   7   8   9 10 11 12 13 14 15 16

—— —— —— —— —— —— —— —— —— ——
17 18 19   20 21 22 23 24 25 26 (from Isaiah 38:8)

Taking Time Backward

Answer

Remember, O Lord, how I have walked before
"PCKCKZCP, M JMPB, FMU G FYTC UYJICB ZCDMPC
   3   23   16   12   9

you faithfully and with wholehearted
WMS DYGRFDSJJW YLB UGRF UFMJCFCYPRCB
       2   7   8   13   1

devotion and have done what is good
BCTMRGML YLB FYTC BMLC UFYR GQ EMMB
  21   4   10   20

in your eyes.
GL WMSP CWCQ." (from Isaiah 38:3)
      15   6

God heard his prayer and added 15 years to his life, plus He delivered Hezekiah and the city from the king of Assyria. God gave a sign so Hezekiah would know He would do as He promised. Replace the letter given with the letter two places before it in the alphabet to find God's sign.

He made the shadow of the sun go back
JG OCFG VJG UJCFQY QH VJG UWP IQ DCEM
24   18   26   5   19 22   11

ten steps on the sundial.
VGP UVGRU QP VJG UWPFKCN. (from Isaiah 38:8)
25   17   14

What does this mean? Use the numbers in both the prayer and sign to fill in the letters.

T i m e w e n t b a c k w a r d
1 2 3 4 5 6 7 8 9 10 11 12 13 14 15 16

t e n d e g r e e s.
17 18 19 20 21 22 23 24 25 26 (from Isaiah 38:8)

Reading the Scrolls
Jeremiah 36:1-32

The Lord told Jeremiah that he should write on a scroll all of the things God had told him concerning Israel, Judah and other nations. So Jeremiah dictated while Baruch wrote down the words. King Jehoiakim responded in an unusual way when Jehudi read the scrolls to him. Use the ruler to find what the king did.

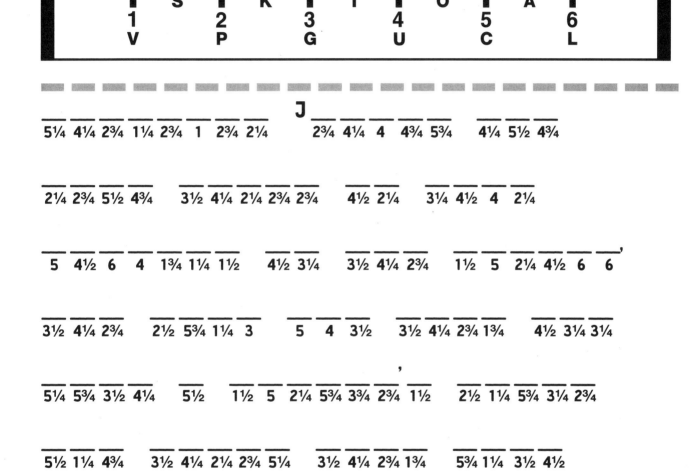

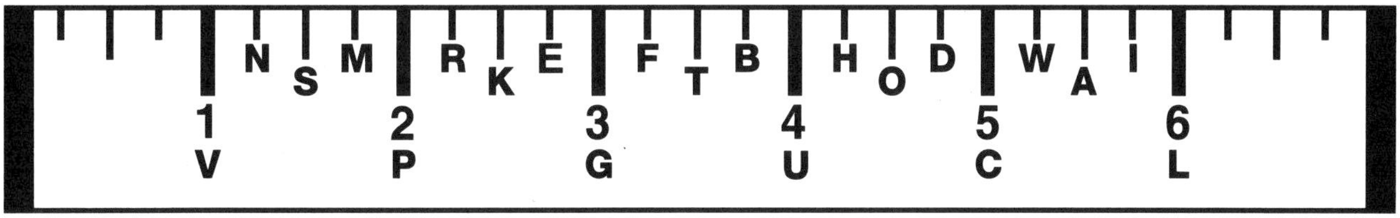

__ __ __ __ __ __ __ __ J __ __ __ __ __ __ __ __
5¼ 4¼ 2¾ 1¼ 2¾ 1 2¾ 2¼   2¾ 4¼ 4 4¾ 5¾ 4¼ 5½ 4¾

__ __ __ __ __ __ __ __ __ __ __ __ __ __ __
2¼ 2¾ 5½ 4¾ 3½ 4¼ 2¼ 2¾ 2¾ 4½ 2¼ 3¼ 4½ 4 2¼

__ __ __ __ __ __ __ __ __ __ __ __ __ __ __ __ __ __ ,
5 4½ 6 4 1¾ 1¼ 1½ 4½ 3¼ 3½ 4¼ 2¾ 1½ 5 2¼ 4½ 6 6

__ __ __ __ __ __ __ __ __ __ __ __ __ __ __ __ __
3½ 4¼ 2¾ 2½ 5¾ 1¼ 3 5 4 3½ 3½ 4¼ 2¾ 1¾ 4½ 3¼ 3¼

__ __ __ __ __ __ __ __ __ __ __ __ , __ __ __ __ __
5¼ 5¾ 3½ 4¼ 5½ 1½ 5 2¼ 5¾ 3¾ 2¾ 1½   2½ 1¼ 5¾ 3¼ 2¾

__ __ __ __ __ __ __ __ __ __ __ __ __ __ __ __
5½ 1¼ 4¾ 3½ 4¼ 2¼ 2¾ 5¼ 3½ 4¼ 2¾ 1¾ 5¾ 1¼ 3½ 4½

__ __ __ __ __ __ __ __ __ __ , __ __ __ __ __ __ __ __
3½ 4¼ 2¾ 3¼ 5¾ 2¼ 2¾ 2 4½ 3½   4 1¼ 3½ 5¾ 6 3½ 4¼ 2¾

__ __ __ __ __ __ __ __ __ __ __ __ __ __ __
2¾ 1¼ 3½ 5¾ 2¼ 2¾ 1½ 5 2¼ 4½ 6 6 5¼ 5½ 1½

__ __ __ __ __ __ __ __ __ __ __ __ __ __ __ .
3¾ 4 2¼ 1¼ 2¾ 4¾ 5¾ 1¼ 3½ 4¼ 2¾ 3¼ 5¾ 2¼ 2¾

— Jeremiah 36:23

Reading the Scrolls

Answer

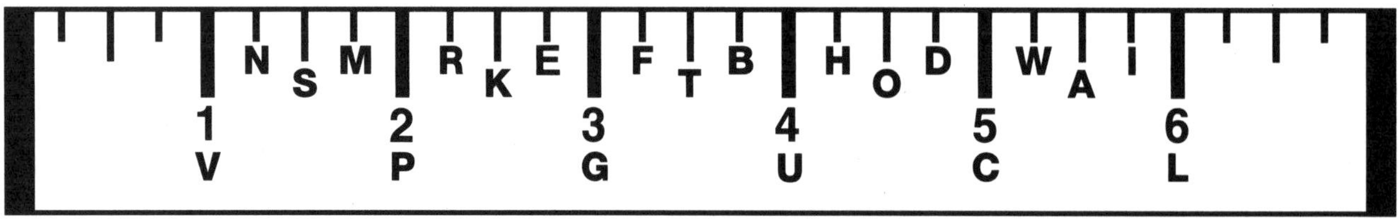

Whenever Jehudi had
5¼ 4¼ 2¾ 1¼ 2¾ 1 2¾ 2¼   2¾ 4¼ 4 4¾ 5¾   4¼ 5½ 4¾

read three or four
2¼ 2¾ 5½ 4¾   3½ 4¼ 2¼ 2¾ 2¾   4½ 2¼   3¼ 4½ 4 2¼

columns of the scroll,
5 4½ 6 4 1¾ 1¼ 1½   4½ 3¼   3½ 4¼ 2¾   1½ 5 2¼ 4½ 6 6

the king cut them off
3½ 4¼ 2¾   2½ 5¾ 1¼ 3   5 4 3½   3½ 4¼ 2¾ 1¾   4½ 3¼ 3¼

with a scribe's knife
5¼ 5¾ 3½ 4¼   5½   1½ 5 2¼ 5¾ 3¾ 2¾ 1½   2½ 1¼ 5¾ 3¼ 2¾

and threw them into
5½ 1¼ 4¾   3½ 4¼ 2¼ 2¾ 5¼   3½ 4¼ 2¾ 1¾   5¾ 1¼ 3½ 4½

the firepot, until the
3½ 4¼ 2¾   3¼ 5¾ 2¼ 2¾ 2 4½ 3½   4 1¼ 3½ 5¾ 6   3½ 4¼ 2¾

entire scroll was
2¾ 1¼ 3½ 5¾ 2¼ 2¾   1½ 5 2¼ 4½ 6 6   5¼ 5½ 1½

burned in the fire.
3¾ 4 2¼ 1¼ 2¾ 4¾   5¾ 1¼   3½ 4¼ 2¾   3¼ 5¾ 2¼ 2¾

– Jeremiah 36:23

52

Hosea's Accusations
Hosea 3-13

Hosea was a prophet who warned the people of Israel that God would punish them for their bad behavior. What were some of the sins Hosea said that Israel committed against God? Find the missing number in each set. The numbers and letters will become your key to answer the question.

2, __, 6, 8 = I   3, __, 9, 12 = R   9, 14, __, 24 = P   1, 2, __, 4 = T

4, 8, __, 16 = O   10, __, 30, 40 = V   6, __, 8, 9 = H   3, 4, __, 6 = S

4, 7, __, 13 = A   6, 7, __, 9 = L   8, __, 18, 23 = G   7, 9, __, 13 = C

14, __, 22, 26 = M   13, 14, __, 16 = N   1, __, 3, 4 = U   7, 8, __, 10 = E

10, 12, __, 16 = D   6, __, 26, 36 = F   9, 13, __, 21 = W

__ __ __ __ __   __ __ __ __ __ __ __   __ __ __ __ __
7 12 5 9 10   10 11 11 2 5 9 14   11 4 20 4 8

__ __ __   __ __ __ __ __ __ __ __ __ __   __ __ __ __ __ __ __
10 15 14   6 9 8 4 13 4 12 2 5   8 9 10 14 9 6 5

__ __   __ __ __ __ __ __ __   __ __ __ __ __ __   __ __ __y
12 16   8 9 10 14 4 15 13   4 5 6 10 9 8   10 17 10

__ __ __ __   __ __ __.   __ __ __ __ __ __   __ __ __
16 6 12 18   13 12 14   4 5 6 10 9 8   7 10 14

__ __ __ __ __ __ __ __   __ __ __   __ __ __
14 9 5 9 6 3 9 14   13 12 14   10 15 14

__ __ __ __ __ __ __ __   __ __ __   __ __ __ __   __ __ __ __ __ __,
6 9 19 8 10 11 9 14   7 4 18   17 4 3 7   4 14 12 8 5

__ __ __ __ __ __ __ __ __
19 12 8 4 3 4 11 10 8

__ __ __ __ __ __ __ __ __ __ __ __ __   __ __ __
10 11 11 12 18 19 8 4 5 7 18 9 15 3   10 15 14

__ __ __ __ __ __   __ __ __ __ __ __,   __ __ __ __   __
5 12 11 4 10 8   5 3 10 3 2 5   10 15 14   10

__ __ __ __ __ __ __ __ __ __ __   __ __ b__   __ __ __ __ __.
14 6 4 20 4 15 13 14 9 5 4 6 9   3 12   9   6 4 11 7

53

Hosea's Accusations

Answer

2, 4, 6, 8 = I

4, 8, 12, 16 = O

4, 7, 10, 13 = A

14, 18, 22, 26 = M

10, 12, 14, 16 = D

3, 6, 9, 12 = R

10, 20, 30, 40 = V

6, 7, 8, 9 = L

13, 14, 15, 16 = N

6, 16, 26, 36 = F

9, 14, 19, 24 = P

6, 7, 8, 9 = H

8, 13, 18, 23 = G

1, 2, 3, 4 = U

9, 13, 17, 21 = W

1, 2, 3, 4 = T

3, 4, 5, 6 = S

7, 9, 11, 13 = C

7, 8, 9, 10 = E

Hosea **accused** **civil**
7 12 5 9 10   10 11 11 2 5 9 14   11 4 20 4 8

and **religious** **leaders**
10 15 14   6 9 8 4 13 4 12 2 5   8 9 10 14 9 6 5

of **leading** **Israel** **away**
12 16   8 9 10 14 4 15 13   4 5 6 10 9 8   10 17 10

from **God.** **Israel** **had**
16 6 12 18   13 12 14   4 5 6 10 9 8   7 10 14

deserted **God** **and**
14 9 5 9 6 3 9 14   13 12 14   10 15 14

replaced **him** **with** **idols,**
6 9 19 8 10 11 9 14   7 4 18   17 4 3 7   4 14 12 8 5

political
19 12 8 4 3 4 11 10 8

accomplishment **and**
10 11 11 12 18 19 8 4 5 7 18 9 15 3   10 15 14

social **status,** **and** **a**
5 12 11 4 10 8   5 3 10 3 2 5   10 15 14   10

driving **desire** **to** **be** **rich.**
14 6 4 20 4 15 13   14 9 5 4 6 9   3 12   9   6 4 11 7

Doubting the Angel of God
Luke 1:5-22

An unusual thing happened to Zechariah before the birth of his son, John. The angel Gabriel came and spoke to Zechariah, but Zechariah doubted his words. What happened? Use the calendar as your code to find out what the angel said after Zechariah doubted.

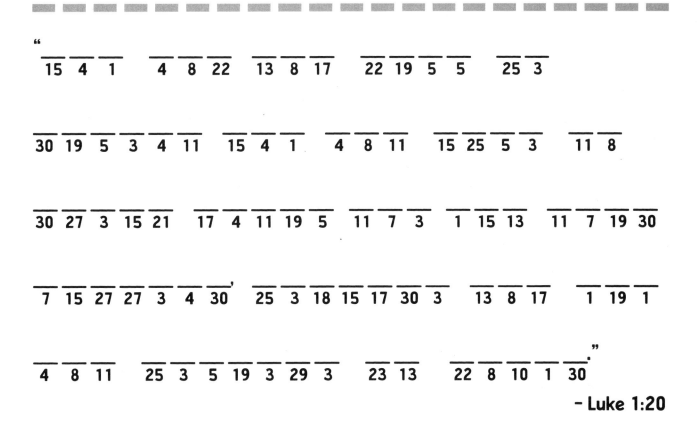

S	M	T	W	TH	F	S
				1d	2	3e
4n	5l	6	7h	8o	9g	10r
11t	12f	13y	14	15a	16	17u
18c	19i	20	21k	22w	23m	24
25b	26	27p	28	29v	30s	31j

"
‾15‾ ‾4‾ ‾1‾   ‾4‾ ‾8‾ ‾22‾   ‾13‾ ‾8‾ ‾17‾   ‾22‾ ‾19‾ ‾5‾ ‾5‾   ‾25‾ ‾3‾

‾30‾ ‾19‾ ‾5‾ ‾3‾ ‾4‾ ‾11‾   ‾15‾ ‾4‾ ‾1‾   ‾4‾ ‾8‾ ‾11‾   ‾15‾ ‾25‾ ‾5‾ ‾3‾   ‾11‾ ‾8‾

‾30‾ ‾27‾ ‾3‾ ‾15‾ ‾21‾   ‾17‾ ‾4‾ ‾11‾ ‾19‾ ‾5‾   ‾11‾ ‾7‾ ‾3‾   ‾1‾ ‾15‾ ‾13‾   ‾11‾ ‾7‾ ‾19‾ ‾30‾

‾7‾ ‾15‾ ‾27‾ ‾27‾ ‾3‾ ‾4‾ ‾30‾'   ‾25‾ ‾3‾ ‾18‾ ‾15‾ ‾17‾ ‾30‾ ‾3‾   ‾13‾ ‾8‾ ‾17‾   ‾1‾ ‾19‾ ‾1‾

‾4‾ ‾8‾ ‾11‾   ‾25‾ ‾3‾ ‾5‾ ‾19‾ ‾3‾ ‾29‾ ‾3‾   ‾23‾ ‾13‾   ‾22‾ ‾8‾ ‾10‾ ‾1‾ ‾30‾."

– Luke 1:20

Doubting the Angel of God

Answer

S	M	T	W	TH	F	S
				1d	2	3e
4n	5l	6	7h	8o	9g	10r
11t	12f	13y	14	15a	16	17u
18c	19i	20	21k	22w	23m	24
25b	26	27p	28	29v	30s	31j

"A n d   n o w   y o u   w i l l   b e
15 4 1   4 8 22   13 8 17   22 19 5 5   25 3

s i l e n t   a n d   n o t   a b l e   t o
30 19 5 3 4 11   15 4 1   4 8 11   15 25 5 3   11 8

s p e a k   u n t i l   t h e   d a y   t h i s
30 27 3 15 21   17 4 11 19 5   11 7 3   1 15 13   11 7 19 30

h a p p e n s,   b e c a u s e   y o u   d i d
7 15 27 27 3 4 30   25 3 18 15 17 30 3   13 8 17   1 19 1

n o t   b e l i e v e   m y   w o r d s."
4 8 11   25 3 5 19 3 29 3   23 13   22 8 10 1 30

– Luke 1:20

A Special Duty
Luke 1:26-38

An angel of the Lord came to Mary to give her amazing news. God had some very special plans for Mary. This news was the beginning of a changed world! Using vowels (a, e, i, o, u), fill in the blanks to reveal the angel's message. Then use the numbered letters beneath the blanks to find Mary's response.

The angel's message:

"D__ n__t b__ __fr__ __d, M__ry, y__ __ h__v__
27   26 6 30 39 10 19 14 32   2 37

f__ __nd f__v__r w__th G__d. Y__ __ w__ll b__ w__th
34   15 9 23 41 21   1 29 18

ch__ld __nd g__v__ b__rth t__ __ s__n, __nd y__ __
35 7 16 22 24 5 4 20 11 17 8

__r__ t__ g__v__ h__m th__ n__m__ J__s__s."
36 13 33 40 25 28 38 3 31 12

- Luke 1:30-31

Mary's response:

"___ ___ ___ ___ ___ ___ ___ ___ ___ ___ ___ ___ ___ ___ ___ ___ ___ ___ , ___ ___ ___ ___ ___ ___ ___ ___ ___ ___ ___ ___ ___ ...
1 2 3 4 5 6 7 8 9 10 11 12 13 14 15 16 17 18

___ ___ ___ ___ ___ ___ ___ ___ ___ ___ ___ ___ ___ ___ ___ ___
19 20 21 22 23 24 25 26 27 28 29 30 31 32 33 34

___ ___ ___ ___ ___ ___ ___ ___ ." *- Luke 1:38*
35 36 37 38 31 39 40 41

57

A Special Duty

Answer

The angel's message:

"D <u>o</u> n<u>o</u>t b<u>e</u> <u>a</u>fr<u>a</u> <u>i</u> d, M<u>a</u>ry, y<u>o</u> u h<u>a</u>v<u>e</u>
  27   26   6   30 39   10   19   32   2 37

f<u>o</u> und f<u>a</u>v<u>o</u>r w<u>i</u>th G<u>o</u>d. Y<u>o</u> u w<u>i</u>ll b<u>e</u> w<u>i</u>th
  34   15   9   23   41 21   1   29   18

ch <u>i</u> ld <u>a</u>nd g<u>i</u>v<u>e</u> b<u>ir</u>th t<u>o</u> <u>a</u> s<u>o</u>n, <u>a</u>nd y<u>o</u> u
35 7   16   22   24   5 4   20 11   17   8

<u>a</u>r<u>e</u> t<u>o</u> g<u>i</u>v<u>e</u> h<u>i</u>m th<u>e</u> n<u>a</u>m<u>e</u> J<u>e</u>s<u>u</u>s."
36 13 33   40 25   28   38   3   31 12

– Luke 1:30-31

Mary's response:

"I am the Lord's servant...
1 2 3   4 5 6   7 8 9 10 11 12 13 14 15 16 17 18

May it be to me as you
19 20 21 22 23 24 25 26 27 28 29 30 31 32 33 34

have said." – Luke 1:38
35 36 37 38   31 39 40 41

58

To See the Messiah
Luke 2:21-32

Simeon was righteous and devout. He had waited many years to see the "consolation of Israel" – the Messiah! What was promised to Simeon through the Holy Spirit? Figure out the code by finding the missing number in each set. Then decipher the promise.

0, _, 22, 33 = D

10, 12, _, 16 = S

5, 6, _, 8 = H

1, _, 5, 7 = A

1, _, 3, 4 = U

6, _, 20, 27 = T

7, 12, _, 22 = L

10, _, 22, 28 = I

3, 4, _, 6 = N

2, 4, _, 8 = F

5, 10, _, 20 = E

2, 3 _, 5 = B

3, 6, _, 12 = W

6, 9, _, 15 = R

6, 8, _, 12 = O

4, _, 12, 16 = C

___ ___   ___ ___ ___ ___ ___   ___ ___ ___   ___ ___ ___
 7 15   9 10 2 17 11   5 10 13   11 16 15

___ ___ ___ ___ ___ ___   ___ ___   ___ ___ ___   ___ ___ ___ ___
 4 15 6 10 12 15   7 15   7 3 11   14 15 15 5

___ ___ ___   ___ ___ ___ ___ ___ ,   ___ ___ ___ ___ ___ ___ .
13 7 15   17 10 12 11 14   8 7 12 16 14 13

– Luke 2:26

To See the Messiah

Answer

0, 11, 22, 33 = D   3, 4, 5, 6 = N

10, 12, 14, 16 = S   2, 4, 6, 8 = F

5, 6, 7, 8 = H   5, 10, 15, 20 = E

1, 3, 5, 7 = A   2, 3, 4, 5 = B

1, 2, 3, 4 = U   3, 6, 9, 12 = W

6, 13, 20, 27 = T   6, 9, 12, 15 = R

7, 12, 17, 22 = L   6, 8, 10, 12 = O

10, 16, 22, 28 = I   4, 8, 12, 16 = C

$\underset{7}{H}\ \underset{15}{e}$ $\underset{9}{w}\ \underset{10}{o}\ \underset{2}{u}\ \underset{17}{l}\ \underset{11}{d}$ $\underset{5}{n}\ \underset{10}{o}\ \underset{13}{t}$ $\underset{11}{d}\ \underset{16}{i}\ \underset{15}{e}$

$\underset{4}{b}\ \underset{15}{e}\ \underset{6}{f}\ \underset{10}{o}\ \underset{12}{r}\ \underset{15}{e}$ $\underset{7}{h}\ \underset{15}{e}$ $\underset{7}{h}\ \underset{3}{a}\ \underset{11}{d}$ $\underset{14}{s}\ \underset{15}{e}\ \underset{15}{e}\ \underset{5}{n}$

$\underset{13}{t}\ \underset{7}{h}\ \underset{15}{e}$ $\underset{17}{L}\ \underset{10}{o}\ \underset{12}{r}\ \underset{11}{d}\text{'}\underset{14}{s}$ $\underset{8}{C}\ \underset{7}{h}\ \underset{12}{r}\ \underset{16}{i}\ \underset{14}{s}\ \underset{13}{t}.$

– Luke 2:26

60

Baptizing Jesus
Matthew 3:13-17

Jesus is God's Son. John the Baptist baptized Jesus in the Jordan River. When John did this, something unique happened that confirmed Jesus as God's Son. Use the code to find out what John and the others witnessed.

A	B	C	D	E	F	G	H	I	J	K	L	M
Z	Y	X	W	V	U	T	S	R	Q	P	O	N

N	O	P	Q	R	S	T	U	V	W	X	Y	Z
M	L	K	J	I	H	G	F	E	D	C	B	A

ZG   GSZG   NLNVMG   SVZEVM   DZH

___ ____ _____ _____ ___

LKVMVW   ZMW   SV   HZD   GSV   HKRIRG

_____, ___ __ ___ ___ _____

LU   TLW   WVHXVMWRMT   ORPV   Z

__ ___ _____ ____ _

WLEV   ZMW   ORTSGRMT   LM   SRN   ZMW

____ ___ _____. __ ___ ___

Z   ELRXV   UILN   SVZEVM   HZRW   GSRH

_ _____ ____ _____ ____, " ____

RH   NB   HLM   DSLN   R   OLEV   DRGS

__ __ ___, ____ _ ____; ____

SRN   R   ZN   DVOO   KOVZHVW

___ _ __ ____ _____."

– Matthew 3:16b-17

Baptizing Jesus

Answer

A	B	C	D	E	F	G	H	I	J	K	L	M
Z	Y	X	W	V	U	T	S	R	Q	P	O	N

N	O	P	Q	R	S	T	U	V	W	X	Y	Z
M	L	K	J	I	H	G	F	E	D	C	B	A

ZG   GSZG   NLNVMG   SVZEVM   DZH
At   that   moment   heaven   was

LKVMVW   ZMW   SV   HZD   GSV   HKRIRG
opened ,   and   he   saw   the   Spirit

LU   TLW   WVHXVMWRMT   ORPV   Z
of   God   descending   like   a

WLEV   ZMW   ORTSGRMT   LM   SRN   ZMW
dove   and   lighting   on   him.   And

Z   ELRXV   UILN   SVZEVM   HZRW   GSRH
a   voice   from   heaven   said, "This

RH   NB   HLM   DSLN   R   OLEV   DRGS
is   my   Son,   whom   I   love;   with

SRN   R   ZN   DVOO   KOVZHVW
him   I   am   well   pleased."

- Matthew 3:16b-17

Born Again?

John 3:1-21

Nicodemus was a member of the Jewish ruling council. He was an educated man who knew Jesus was God's Son. Jesus explained to Nicodemus that he must be born again to enter into heaven. What did Nicodemus say when Jesus told him? Use the letters in EDUCATED to fill in the missing letters in the verse from John 3:4.

"H o w _ _ n _ m_n b_ b o r n wh_ n h_ i s o l_ ?
33 16   40 9 63 20 53 10   59 4   49 6 31 43   17 64   56 61 11 39 66 27

S _ r _ l y h_ _ _ nno_ _ n _ _ r _ s _ _ o n _
45 26 7 41 38 50   18 34 1   54 32 19 23 65 14 44 51 67 62

_ im_ i n _ o h i s mo_ h_ r's womb _ o b_ b o r n!"
47 22 48 24 12 36 52 37 13 55   2 25 58 29 46 21   35 5   15 42 3 60 30 57 28 8

Now use the letters above the numbers to find what lesson Jesus was teaching Nicodemus that night.

_ _ _ _ _ _ _ _ _g_ _ _ _ _ _ _ _ _ _v_
1 2   3 4   5 6 7 8   9 10 11 12   13 14   15 16   17 18 19

_ _p_ _ _ _ _ _ _ _ _ _ _ _ _ _, _ _ _ _
20   21 22 23 24 25 26 10 27   28 29 30 13 31 32 33   34 35 36   18

p_ _ _ _ _ _ _ _ _ _. _p_ _ _ _ _ _ _
37 38 39 22 40 9 41   42 43 44   45 24 46 11 47 26 20 27

_ _ _ _ _ _ _ _ _ _ _ _ _ _ _ _ _g_
7 48 49 13 28 25 50   51 52 53 54 55   36 56 23 57 26 58

_ _ _ _ _v_ _g_ _ _ J_ _ _ _ _ _
59 60 41 11 61 22 62   24 63   64 39 26 21   65 45

_ _ _ _ _ _v_ _ _.
38 66 26 31   14 65 13 67 46   (from John 3:1-21)

Born Again?

Answer

"How <u>c a</u> n <u>a</u> m<u>a</u>n b<u>e</u> born wh<u>e</u>n h<u>e</u> is o l<u>d</u>?
33 16   40 9 63 20 53 10   59 4 49 6 31 43   17 64   56 61 11 39 66 27

<u>S</u> <u>u</u>r<u>el</u> y h<u>e</u> <u>c</u> <u>a</u>nno<u>t</u> <u>en</u>t <u>er</u> <u>a</u> s <u>e</u>c<u>o</u>n<u>d</u>
45 26 7 41 38 50   18 34 1   54 32 19 23 65 14 44 51 67 62

<u>t</u> im<u>e</u> i n<u>t</u>o his mo<u>th</u>e<u>r</u>'s womb <u>t</u>o b<u>e</u> b o r n!"
47 22 48 24 12 36 52 37 13 55   2 25 58 29 46 21   35 5   15 42 3 60 30 57 28 8

Now use the letters above the numbers to find what lesson Jesus was teaching
Nicodemus that night.

<u>T</u>o <u>b</u>e <u>b o r n</u> <u>a</u>g<u>a</u>in is to h<u>a</u>ve
1 2 3 4 5 6 7 8 9 10 11 12 13 14 15 16 17 18 19

<u>a</u> <u>s</u>p<u>i r i t u a l</u> <u>r e b i r t h,</u> <u>n o t</u> <u>a</u>
20 21 22 23 24 25 26 10 27 28 29 30 13 31 32 33 34 35 36 18

<u>p</u>h<u>y s i c a l</u> <u>o n e</u>. <u>S</u>p<u>i r i t u a l</u>
37 38 39 22 40 9 41 42 43 44 45 24 46 11 47 26 20 27

<u>r e b i r t h</u> <u>c o m e s</u> <u>t h r o u g h</u>
7 48 49 13 28 25 50 51 52 53 54 55 36 56 23 57 26 58

<u>b e l i e</u>v<u>i n</u>g <u>i n</u> <u>J e s u s</u> <u>a s</u>
59 60 41 11 61 22 62 24 63 64 39 26 21 65 45

<u>y o u r</u> <u>S</u>a<u>v i o r</u>.
38 66 26 31 14 65 13 67 46

(from John 3:1-21)

Jairus's Problem
Mark 5:21-43

Jairus was a synagogue ruler who had a terrible problem. He went to Jesus to get help with his problem. Do the math to find the code, then write the letters on the blanks to find the problem.

Add 8 to each number:

A	B	C	D	E	F	G	H	I	J	K	L	M
17	77	54	38	21	62	35	88	7	82	91	14	46

— — — — — — — — — — — — —

Subtract 8 from each number:

N	O	P	Q	R	S	T	U	V	W	X	Y	Z
11	26	53	44	15	81	41	32	50	36	47	67	23

— — — — — — — — — — — — —

What was Jairus's special problem?

— — —   — — — — — —   — — — —   — — —
96 15 73   22 15 33 33 22 29   43 15 7 22   28 25 73

— — — —   — — — — .
42 29 7 59   73 15 62 99

What happened before Jesus got to Jairus's home?

— — — — — —   — — —   — — — —   — — —
90 25 15 7 24 73   28 25 73   33 18 22 46   96 15 73

— — — — — — — —   — — —   — — — — .
46 25 24 43 96 33 29 7   96 25 46   46 15 29 46

Jesus told Jairus to ignore what he had been told. What did Jesus tell Jairus to do instead?

"— — — — ,   — —   — — — — — — ;   — — — —
46 18 3 33   85 29   25 70 7 25 15 46   90 24 73 33

— — — — — — — ."
85 29 22 15 29 42 29

(from Mark 5:21-43)

Jairus's Problem

Answer

Add 8 to each number:

A	B	C	D	E	F	G	H	I	J	K	L	M
17	77	54	38	21	62	35	88	7	82	91	14	46
25	85	62	46	29	70	43	96	15	90	99	22	54

Subtract 8 from each number:

N	O	P	Q	R	S	T	U	V	W	X	Y	Z
11	26	53	44	15	81	41	32	50	36	47	67	23
3	18	45	36	7	72	33	24	42	28	39	59	15

- -

What was Jairus's special problem?

H i s   l i t t l e   g i r l   w a s
96 15 73   22 15 33 33 22 29   43 15 7 22   28 25 73

v e r y   s i c k.
42 29 7 59   73 15 62 99

What happened before Jesus got to Jairus's home?

J a i r u s   w a s   t o l d   h i s
90 25 15 7 24 73   28 25 73   33 18 22 46   96 15 73

d a u g h t e r   h a d   d i e d.
46 25 24 43 96 33 29 7   96 25 46   46 15 29 46

Jesus told Jairus to ignore what he had been told. What did Jesus tell Jairus to do instead?

"D o n't   b e   a f r a i d; j u s t
46 18 3 33   85 29   25 70 7 25 15 46   90 24 73 33

b e l i e v e."
85 29 22 15 29 42 29

(from Mark 5:21-43)

Mary Magdalene's Miracle
Luke 8:1-2

Mary Magdalene became a faithful follower of Jesus after a dramatic event in her life. What was this event? Go through each line of the alphabet shown to see which letter is missing. Write that letter on the line to find this life-changing incident.

ABCDEFGHIJKLMNOPQRTUVWXYZ ___
ABCDEFGIJKLMNOPQRSTUVWXYZ ___
ABCDFGHIJKLMNOPQRSTUVWXYZ ___

ABCDEFGHIJKLMNOPQRSTUVXYZ ___
BCDEFGHIJKLMNOPQRSTUVWXYZ ___
ABCDEFGHIJKLMNOPQRTUVWXYZ ___

ABCDEFGIJKLMNOPQRSTUVWXYZ ___
ABCDFGHIJKLMNOPQRSTUVWXYZ ___
BCDEFGHIJKLMNOPQRSTUVWXYZ ___

ABCDEFGHIJKMNOPQRSTUVWXYZ ___
ABCDFGHIJKLMNOPQRSTUVWXYZ ___
ABCEFGHIJKLMNOPQRSTUVWXYZ ___

ABCDEFGHIJKLMNPQRSTUVWXYZ ___
ABCDEGHIJKLMNOPQRSTUVWXYZ ___

ABCDFGHIJKLMNOPQRSTUVWXYZ ___
ABCDEFGHIJKLMNOPQRSTUWXYZ ___
ABCDEFGHJKLMNOPQRSTUVWXYZ ___
ABCDEFGHIJKMNOPQRSTUVWXYZ ___

ABCDEFGHIJKLMNOPQRTUVWXYZ ___
ABCDEFGHIJKLMNOQRSTUVWXYZ ___

ABCDEFGHJKLMNOPQRSTUVWXYZ ___
ABCDEFGHIJKLMNOPQSTUVWXYZ ___
ABCDEFGHJKLMNOPQRSTUVWXYZ ___
ABCDEFGHIJKLMNOPQRSUVWXYZ ___

ABCDEFGHIJKLMNOPQRTUVWXYZ ___.

ABCDEFGHIJKLMNOPQRTUVWXYZ ___
ABCDFGHIJKLMNOPQRSTUVWXYZ ___
ABCDEFGHIJKLMNOPQRSTUWXYZ ___
ABCDFGHIJKLMNOPQRSTUVWXYZ ___
ABCDEFGHIJKLMOPQRSTUVWXYZ ___

ABCEFGHIJKLMNOPQRSTUVWXYZ ___
ABCDFGHIJKLMNOPQRSTUVWXYZ ___
ABCDEFGHIJKLNOPQRSTUVWXYZ ___
ABCDEFGHIJKLMNPQRSTUVWXYZ ___
ABCDEFGHIJKLMOPQRSTUVWXYZ ___
ABCDEFGHIJKLMNOPQRTUVWXYZ ___

ABCDEFGIJKLMNOPQRSTUVWXYZ ___
BCDEFGHIJKLMNOPQRSTUVWXYZ ___
ABCEFGHIJKLMNOPQRSTUVWXYZ ___

ACDEFGHIJKLMNOPQRSTUVWXYZ ___
ABCDFGHIJKLMNOPQRSTUVWXYZ ___
ABCDFGHIJKLMNOPQRSTUVWXYZ ___
ABCDEFGHIJKLMOPQRSTUVWXYZ ___

ABDEFGHIJKLMNOPQRSTUVWXYZ ___
BCDEFGHIJKLMNOPQRSTUVWXYZ ___
ABCDEFGHIJKLMNOPQRTUVWXYZ ___
ABCDEFGHIJKLMNOPQRSUVWXYZ ___

ABCDEFGHIJKLMNPQRSTUVWXYZ ___
ABCDEFGHIJKLMNOPQRSTVWXYZ ___
ABCDEFGHIJKLMNOPQRSUVWXYZ ___

ABCDEGHIJKLMNOPQRSTUVWXYZ ___
ABCDEFGHIJKLMNOPQSTUVWXYZ ___
ABCDEFGHIJKLMNPQRSTUVWXYZ ___
ABCDEFGHIJKLNOPQRSTUVWXYZ ___

ABCDEFGIJKLMNOPQRSTUVWXYZ ___
ABCDFGHIJKLMNOPQRSTUVWXYZ ___
ABCDEFGHIJKLMNOPQSTUVWXYZ ___.

(from Luke 8:1-2)

Mary Magdalene's Miracle

Answer

ABCDEFGHIJKLMNOPQRTUVWXYZ	S	ABCEFGHIJKLMNOPQRSTUVWXYZ	D
ABCDEFGIJKLMNOPQRSTUVWXYZ	H	ABCDFGHIJKLMNOPQRSTUVWXYZ	E
ABCDFGHIJKLMNOPQRSTUVWXYZ	E	ABCDEFGHIJKLNOPQRSTUVWXYZ	M
		ABCDEFGHIJKLMNPQRSTUVWXYZ	O
ABCDEFGHIJKLMNOPQRSTUVXYZ	W	ABCDEFGHIJKLMOPQRSTUVWXYZ	N
BCDEFGHIJKLMNOPQRSTUVWXYZ	A	ABCDEFGHIJKLMNOPQRTUVWXYZ	S
ABCDEFGHIJKLMNOPQRTUVWXYZ	S		
		ABCDEFGIJKLMNOPQRSTUVWXYZ	H
ABCDEFGIJKLMNOPQRSTUVWXYZ	H	BCDEFGHIJKLMNOPQRSTUVWXYZ	A
ABCDFGHIJKLMNOPQRSTUVWXYZ	E	ABCEFGHIJKLMNOPQRSTUVWXYZ	D
BCDEFGHIJKLMNOPQRSTUVWXYZ	A		
ABCDEFGHIJKMNOPQRSTUVWXYZ	L	ACDEFGHIJKLMNOPQRSTUVWXYZ	B
ABCDFGHIJKLMNOPQRSTUVWXYZ	E	ABCDFGHIJKLMNOPQRSTUVWXYZ	E
ABCEFGHIJKLMNOPQRSTUVWXYZ	D	ABCDFGHIJKLMNOPQRSTUVWXYZ	E
		ABCDEFGHIJKLMOPQRSTUVWXYZ	N
ABCDEFGHIJKLMNPQRSTUVWXYZ	O		
ABCDEGHIJKLMNOPQRSTUVWXYZ	F	ABDEFGHIJKLMNOPQRSTUVWXYZ	C
		BCDEFGHIJKLMNOPQRSTUVWXYZ	A
ABCDFGHIJKLMNOPQRSTUVWXYZ	E	ABCDEFGHIJKLMNOPQRTUVWXYZ	S
ABCDEFGHIJKLMNOPQRSTUWXYZ	V	ABCDEFGHIJKLMNOPQRSUVWXYZ	T
ABCDEFGHJKLMNOPQRSTUVWXYZ	I		
ABCDEFGHIJKMNOPQRSTUVWXYZ	L	ABCDEFGHIJKLMNPQRSTUVWXYZ	O
		ABCDEFGHIJKLMNOPQRSTVWXYZ	U
ABCDEFGHIJKLMNOPQRTUVWXYZ	S	ABCDEFGHIJKLMNOPQRSUVWXYZ	T
ABCDEFGHIJKLMNOQRSTUVWXYZ	P		
ABCDEFGHJKLMNOPQRSTUVWXYZ	I	ABCDEGHIJKLMNOPQRSTUVWXYZ	F
ABCDEFGHIJKLMNOPQSTUVWXYZ	R	ABCDEFGHIJKLMNOPQSTUVWXYZ	R
ABCDEFGHJKLMNOPQRSTUVWXYZ	I	ABCDEFGHIJKLMNPQRSTUVWXYZ	O
ABCDEFGHIJKLMNOPQRSUVWXYZ	T	ABCDEFGHIJKLNOPQRSTUVWXYZ	M
ABCDEFGHIJKLMNOPQRTUVWXYZ	S.		
		ABCDEFGIJKLMNOPQRSTUVWXYZ	H
ABCDEFGHIJKLMNOPQRTUVWXYZ	S	ABCDFGHIJKLMNOPQRSTUVWXYZ	E
ABCDFGHIJKLMNOPQRSTUVWXYZ	E	ABCDEFGHIJKLMNOPQSTUVWXYZ	R.
ABCDEFGHIJKLMNOPQRSTUWXYZ	V		
ABCDFGHIJKLMNOPQRSTUVWXYZ	E		
ABCDEFGHIJKLMOPQRSTUVWXYZ	N		

(from Luke 8:1-2)

68

A Beggar's Request
Mark 10:46-52

Bartimaeus was a beggar. Jesus passed by him on His way through the city of Jericho. Bartimaeus had a special problem. Use the eye chart to find the answers to the questions about Bartimaeus.

```
        A       Z       B       D       I
        9       1       15      19      8

    J       H       N       O       Q       L       S
    18      10      2       14      7       20      24

  T       W       V       P       C       E       G       M
  17      23      6       11      3       21      13      26

          Y       F       K       R       U       X
          5       25      16      22      12      4
```

1. What was Bartimaeus's problem?

___ ___   ___ ___ ___   ___ ___ ___ ___ ___.
10 21   23 9 24   15 20 8   2 19

2. What did he say to Jesus as He passed him?

"
___ ___ ___ ___ ___, ___ ___ ___ ___ ___ ___ ___ ___ ___ ___, ___ ___ ___ ___
18 21 24 12 24   24 14 2   14 25 19 9 6 8 19   10 9 6 21

___ ___ ___ ___ ___ ___ ___ ___ ___!"
26 21 22 3 5   14 2   26 21

3. What did Jesus ask Bartimaeus?

"
___ ___ ___ ___ ___ ___ ___ ___ ___ ___ ___ ___ ___ ___ ___ ___ ___ ___ ___
23 10 9 17   19 14   5 14 12   23 9 2 17   26 21   17 14   19 14

___ ___ ___ ___ ___ ___?"
25 14 22   5 14 12

4. What was Bartimaeus' request?

"
___ ___ ___ ___ ___, ___ ___ ___ ___ ___ ___ ___ ___ ___ ___."
22 9 15 15 8   8   23 9 2 17   17 14   24 21 21

5. How did Jesus respond?

"
___ ___, ___ ___ ___ ___ ___ ___ ___ ___ ___ ___ ___ ___
13 14   5 14 12 22   25 9 8 17 10   10 9 24

___ ___ ___ ___ ___ ___ ___ ___ ___."
10 21 9 20 21 19   5 14 12

(from Mark 10:46-52)

A Beggar's Request

Answer

A	Z	B	D	I
9	1	15	19	8

J	H	N	O	Q	L	S
18	10	2	14	7	20	24

T	W	V	P	C	E	G	M
17	23	6	11	3	21	13	26

Y	F	K	R	U	X
5	25	16	22	12	4

---

1. What was Bartimaeus's problem?

He was blind.
10 21   23 9 24   15 20 8 2 19

2. What did he say to Jesus as He passed him?

"Jesus, Son of David, have
18 21 24 12 24   24 14 2   14 25   19 9 6 8 19   10 9 6 21

mercy on me!"
26 21 22 3 5   14 2   26 21

3. What did Jesus ask Bartimaeus?

"What do you want me to do
23 10 9 17   19 14   5 14 12   23 9 2 17   26 21   17 14   19 14

for you?"
25 14 22   5 14 12

4. What was Bartimaeus' request?

"Rabbi, I want to see."
22 9 15 15 8   8   23 9 2 17   17 14   24 21 21

5. How did Jesus respond?

"Go, your faith has
13 14   5 14 12 22   25 9 8 17 10   10 9 24

healed you."
10 21 9 20 21 19   5 14 12

(from Mark 10:46-52)

Much to Be Done!

Luke 10:38-42

Luke 10:38-42 shares a story of two sisters. Mary stops what she's doing to listen to Jesus. Her sister, Martha, frets over the many things that need to be done for His visit. Use the word bank to find Jesus' surprising reaction to their behavior. Match the numbered word to the space where it belongs.

1. chosen	2. upset	3. worried	4. away	5. will	6. Martha
7. needed	8. Martha	9. thing	10. her	11. about	12. are
13. taken	14. better	15. Mary	16. many	17. and	18. things
19. and	20. only	21. has	22. it	23. be	24. from
25. is	26. but	27. one	28. what	29. not	30. is
31. you					

"_____, _____ . . . _____ _____ _____ _____
   8   6   31   12   3   17

_____ _____ _____ _____, _____ _____ _____
  2   11   16   18   26   20   27

_____ _____ _____ . _____ _____ _____ _____
  9   25   7   15   21   1   28

_____ _____ _____, _____ _____ _____ _____
  30   14   19   22   5   29   23

_____ _____ _____ _____ ."   - Luke 10:41-42
  13   4   24   10

What can we learn from this lesson? Use the following letters to fill in the blanks of the missing letters in each word to find out. (Use each letter only once.)

S O T S D J S C L T F R

__esu__   __hris__   __houl__   be   __irs__

in   __u__   __ive__ .

Much to Be Done!

Answer

1. chosen   2. upset   3. worried   4. away   5. will   6. Martha

7. needed   8. Martha   9. thing   10. her   11. about   12. are

13. taken   14. better   15. Mary   16. many   17. and   18. things

19. and   20. only   21. has   22. it   23. be   24. from

25. is   26. but   27. one   28. what   29. not   30. is

31. you

"Martha , Martha … you are worried and
8   6   31   12   3   17

upset about many things but only one
2   11   16   18   26   20   27

thing is needed. Mary has chosen what
9   25   7   15   21   1   28

is better , and it will not be
30   14   19   22   5   29   23

taken away from her ."   – Luke 10:41-42
13   4   24   10

What can we learn from this lesson? Use the following letters to fill in the blanks of the missing letters in each word to find out.

S O T S D J S C L T F R

Jesu_s_ _C_hris_t_ _s_houl_d_ be _f_irs_t_ in _o_u_r_ _l_ive_s_.

72

Faith and Doubt
Matthew 14:22-32

Peter, also called Simon, was one of Jesus' first disciples. He is noted for many things. Peter followed Jesus to become one of His "fishers of men." Peter was the one who denied Jesus three times before the cock crowed when Jesus was arrested. He is also noted for his great faith followed by doubt. What episode demonstrates Peter's difficulty with faith (1) and what did Jesus say to him about it (2)? Fill in the missing vowels in each word (a, e, i, o, u, y). Then decide which word in each set does not belong. Write those words on the lines provided to answer the question.

1. Sn__w   P__t__r   __c__

2. w__lk__d   c__ff__ __   t__ __

3. s__ng   m__s__c   __n

4. c__ts   d__gs   w__t__r

5. r__d   y__ __   gr__ __n

6. __f   st__ __l   ch__ __r

7. l__ttl__   c__r   b__c__cl__

8. h__y   str__w   f__ __th

9. wh__   p__p__r   p__nc__l

10. m__ __n   st__rs   d__d

11. y__ __   tr__ __s   l__ __v__s

12. sh__ __   s__ck   d__ __bt

1. _____ _____ _____ _____.
    1   2   3   4

2. "_____ _____ _____ _____
    5   6   7   8

_____ _____ _____ _____?"
   9   10   11   12

(from Matthew 14:29-31)

73

Faith and Doubt

Answer

1. Sn<u>o</u>w	P<u>et e</u>r	<u>i</u>c<u>e</u>
2. w<u>a</u>lk<u>e</u>d	c<u>o</u>ff<u>e</u> <u>e</u>	t<u>e</u> <u>a</u>
3. s<u>o</u>ng	m<u>us i</u>c	<u>o</u>n
4. c<u>a</u>ts	d<u>o</u>gs	w<u>a</u>t<u>e</u>r
5. r<u>e</u>d	y<u>o</u> u	gr<u>e</u> <u>e</u>n
6. <u>o</u>f	st<u>o</u> <u>o</u>l	ch<u>a</u> i r
7. l<u>i</u>ttl<u>e</u>	c<u>a</u>r	b <u>i</u>c<u>y</u>cl<u>e</u>
8. h<u>a</u>y	str<u>a</u>w	f<u>a</u> <u>i</u>th
9. wh<u>y</u>	p<u>a</u>p<u>e</u>r	p<u>e</u>nc<u>i</u>l
10. m<u>o</u> <u>o</u>n	st<u>a</u>rs	d<u>i</u>d
11. y<u>o</u> u	tr<u>e</u> <u>e</u>s	l<u>e</u> av<u>e</u>s
12. sh<u>o</u> <u>e</u>	s<u>o</u>ck	d<u>o</u> <u>u</u>bt

---

1. <u>Peter</u> <u>walked</u> <u>on</u> <u>water</u> .
   1   2   3   4

2. " <u>You</u> <u>of</u> <u>little</u> <u>faith</u>
    5   6   7   8

<u>why</u> <u>did</u> <u>you</u> <u>doubt</u> ?"
 9   10   11   12

(from Matthew 14:29-31)

An Awful Deed
Matthew 26:14-56; 27:1-5

One of the 12 disciples betrayed Jesus. His actions ultimately led to Jesus' arrest and crucifixion. Some clues to this disciple's name are given below. Use the calculator keys to fill in the blanks to find the clues, then unscramble the circled letters to figure out the name of the disciple.

Who Am I?

___ ___ ___ ___ ___   ___ ___ ___ ___ ___ ___ ___ ___

(from Matthew 26-27)

An Awful Deed

Answer

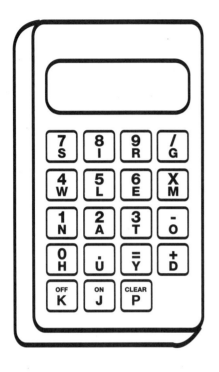

He went to the chief
0 6   4 6 1 3   3 -   3 0 6   0 8 6

priests and asked
clear 9 8 6 7 3 7   2 1 +   2 7 off 6 +

what they would give
4 0 2 3   3 0 6 =   4 - . 5 +   / 8 6

if he handed him over.
8   0 6   0 2 1 + 6 +   0 8 X   - 6 9

At the Lord's Supper,
2 3   3 0 6   5 - 9 + 7   7 . clear clear 6 9

when Jesus said one
4 0 6 1   on 6 7 . 7   7 2 8 +   - 1 6

of the twelve would
-   3 0 6   3 4 6 5 6   4 - . 5 +

betray Him, this person said,
6 3 9 2 =   0 8 X 3 0 8 7 clear 6 9 7 - 1   7 2 8 +

"Surely not I, rabbi?" In the garden
7 . 9 6 5 =   1 - 3 8   9 2 8   8 1   3 0 6   / 2 9 + 6 1

of Gethsemane he said, "The one I
- / 6 3 0 7 6 X 2 1 6   0 6   7 2 8 +   3 0 6   - 1 6 8

kiss is the man; arrest him." He
off 8 7 7   8 7   3 0 6   X 2 1   2 9 9 6 7 3   0 8 X   0 6

threw the money into the temple
3 0 9 6 4   3 0 6   X - 1 6 =   8 1 3 -   3 0 6   3 6 X clear 5 6

and left and caused his own death.
2 1 +   5 6 3   2 1 +   2 . 7 6 +   0 8 7   - 4 1 + 6 2 3 0

Who Am I?

Judas Iscariot (from Matthew 26-27)

Less Known, Not Less Important
Acts 1:12-14

Of the 12 disciples, some receive less attention in the Bible than others. But there is no doubt that Jesus knew the special capabilities of everyone He called to be a disciple. To find the name of one of the lesser-known disciples, find the numbered letter in each word. Then add or subtract that letter's place in the alphabet to find the new letter.

A B C D E F G H I J K L M N O P Q R S T U V W X Y Z

Example: Road #4 + 6 = J (D 4th letter in the word + 6 more letters = J)

Word	Clue	Answer
Herald	#3 - 16 =	___
Question	#5 - 19 =	___
Living	#6 + 11 =	___
Political	#2 + 5 =	___
Succeed	#1 - 11 =	___
Evangelize	#9 - 11 =	___
Nativity	#4 + 3 =	___
Receive	#6 - 7 =	___
Clever	#2 + 1 =	___
Float	#5 - 15 =	___
Thrill	#3 + 5 =	___

What were the disciples doing in the Upper Room after Jesus' ascension?

Word	Clue	Answer
Judge	#1 + 6 =	___
Minute	#4 - 3 =	___
Golden	#6 - 13 =	___
Illusion	#2 + 13 =	___
Discovery	#8 - 9 =	___
Knowledge	#5 + 2 =	___
Lighthouse	#7 - 8 =	___

(from Acts 1:12-14)

Less Known, Not Less Important

Answer

A B C D E F G H I J K L M N O P Q R S T U V W X Y Z

Herald	#3 - 16 =	B
Question	#5 - 19 =	A
Living	#6 + 11 =	R
Political	#2 + 5 =	T
Succeed	#1 - 11 =	H
Evangelize	#9 - 11 =	O
Nativity	#4 + 3 =	L
Receive	#6 - 7 =	O
Clever	#2 + 1 =	M
Float	#5 - 15 =	E
Thrill	#3 + 5 =	W

What were they doing in the Upper Room?

Judge	#1 + 6 =	P
Minute	#4 - 3 =	R
Golden	#6 - 13 =	A
Illusion	#2 + 13 =	Y
Discovery	#8 - 9 =	I
Knowledge	#5 + 2 =	N
Lighthouse	#7 - 8 =	G

(from Acts 1:12-14)

God Will Make Clean
Acts 10

Cornelius was a God-fearing man known by many Romans and Jews. He had a vision that he should speak with Peter about the Gospel. So he told two of his servants to go get Peter. Meanwhile, Peter also had a vision that somewhat confused him. When the servants came to get Peter, he went with them even though Cornelius was a Gentile and considered unclean. What did God say to Peter? What was God teaching Peter through his confusing vision and the visit to Cornelius?

What did God say to Peter? Begin with the first O and place every other vowel on the spaces with number signs (#). Then write every other consonant on the remaining spaces, beginning with the letter D.

O A O E A I A O Y U I A I E U I E O A U O A A E A I E O E U A A D B N C T D C F L G L H
N J T K H L N M G N M P P Q R R T S H T T V G W D X H Z S B M C D D C F L G N H

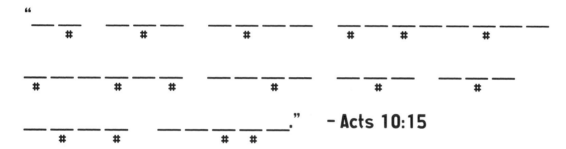

" ___ ___   ___ ___   ___ ___ ___   ___ ___ ___ ___   ___ ___ ___
      #   #   #   #   #   #

___ ___ ___ ___   ___ ___ ___   ___ ___ ___   ___ ___ ___   ___ ___ ___
    #   #   #   #   #

___ ___ ___   ___ ___ ___ ___ .” – Acts 10:15
    #   #   #   #

What was God teaching Peter? Write every other vowel beginning with the first A on the spaces with a star (★). Then write every other consonant on the remaining spaces, beginning with T.

A A O E O I E O O U O A A E O I I O I U U A A E E I E O O U E A E E Y I A O I U O A O E
E I A O I U A A O E A I I O I U T B H C T D G F D G D H S J N K T L S M H N W P F Q
V R R S T T S V M W B X T Z C B C C P D T F S G M H N J F K R L M M V N R P N
Q T R N S W T H V F W R X H Z M B N C D T D F W G H H T J S K R I G M H N T P

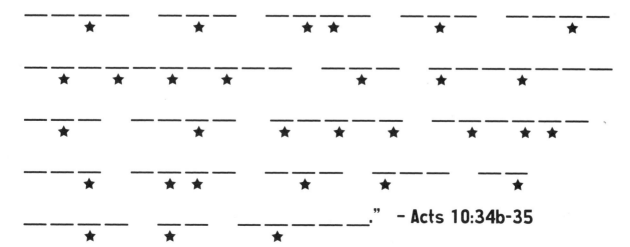

___ ___ ___ ___   ___ ___ ___ ___   ___ ___ ___   ___ ___ ___   ___ ___ ___ ___
          ★   ★   ★   ★   ★   ★

___ ___ ___ ___ ___   ___ ___ ___ ___   ___ ___ ___   ___ ___ ___ ___
    ★   ★   ★   ★   ★   ★   ★

___ ___ ___ ___   ___ ___ ___ ___   ___ ___ ___ ___ ___   ___ ___ ___ ___ ___
    ★   ★   ★   ★   ★   ★   ★

___ ___ ___   ___ ___ ___ ___   ___ ___ ___   ___ ___ ___ ___
          ★   ★   ★   ★   ★   ★

___ ___ ___   ___ ___   ___ ___ ___ ___ .” – Acts 10:34b-35
    ★   ★   ★

79

God Will Make Clean

Answer

What did God say to Peter? Begin with O and place every other vowel on the spaces with a number sign (#). Then write every other consonant on the remaining spaces, beginning with the letter D.

O A O E A I A O Y U I A I E U I E O A U O A A E A I E O E U A A D B N C T D C F L G L H
N J T K H L N M G N M P P Q R R T S H T T V G W D X H Z S B M C D D C F L G N H

"Do not call anything
impure that God has
made clean." – Acts 10:15

What was God teaching Peter? Write every other vowel beginning with the first A on the spaces with a star (★). Then write every other consonant on the remaining spaces, beginning with T.

A A O E O I E O O U O A A E O I I O I U U A A E E I E O O U E A E E Y I A O I U O A O E
E I A O I U A A O E A I I O I U T B H C T D G F D G D H S J N K T L S M H N W P F Q
V R R S T T S V M W B X T Z C B C C P D T F S G M H N J F K R L M M V N R P N
Q T R N S W T H V F W R X H Z M B N C D T D F W G H H T J S K R I G M H N T P

That God does not show
favoritism but accepts
men from every nation
who fear him and do
what is right." – Acts 10:34b-35

Unusual Behavior
Acts 16:16-33

Silas, a Christian, traveled with Paul to spread the Good News. On one occasion Paul and Silas were jailed because they were preaching. A guard at the jail watched them carefully. Paul and Silas did something unusual considering they were locked in jail, and then something even more unusual happened. Use the radio dial to find what Paul and Silas did and the result of their actions.

FM 88 h 92 n 96 d 100 a 104 s 108 o

AM 550 t 650 r 800 l 1000 c 1300 i 1600 e

① ② ③ ④
⑤ ⑥ ⑦ ⑧

___ ___ __y w___ ___ ___
am550 fm88 am1600 am1600 am650 am1600

p___ ___y ___ ___g ___ ___ ___
am650 fm100 am1300 fm92 fm100 fm92 fm96

___ ___ ___g___ ___g
fm104 am1300 fm92 am1300 fm92

___ym___ ___ ___ ___
fm88 fm92 fm104 am550 fm108

G___ ___. (from Acts 10:25)
fm108 fm96

___ v___ ___ ___ ___ ___ ___
fm100 am1300 fm108 am800 am1600 fm92 am550

___ ___ ___ ___ ___qu __k___
am1600 fm100 am650 am550 fm88 fm100 am1600

___ ___u___ ___ ___ ___ ___
am1000 fm100 fm104 am1600 fm96 am550 fm88 am1600

f___u___ ___ ___ ___ ___ ___ ___   ___f ___ ___ ___
fm108 fm92 fm96 fm100 am550 am1300 fm108 fm92 fm104   fm108   am550 fm88 am1600

p___ ___ ___ ___ ___   ___ ___   ___ ___ ___k___   ___ ___ ___
am650 am1300 fm104 fm108 fm92   am550 fm108   fm104 fm88 fm100 am1600   fm100 fm92 fm96

___ ___ ___   ___ ___ ___   p___ ___ ___ ___ ___
fm100 am800 am800   am550 fm88 am1600   am650 am1300 fm104 fm108 fm92

___ ___ ___ ___ ___   ___p___ ___ ___ ___   ___ ___ ___
fm96 fm108 fm108 am650 fm104   fm108 am1600 fm92 am1600 fm96   fm100 fm92 fm96

___v ___ ___yb___ ___y'___   ___ ___ ___ ___ ___ ___
am1600 am1600 am650 fm108 fm96 fm104   am1000 fm88 fm100 am1300 fm92 fm104

___ ___m___   ___ ___ ___ ___ ___.   (from Acts 10:26)
am1000 fm100 am1600   am800 fm108 fm108 fm104 am1600

81

Unusual Behavior

Answer

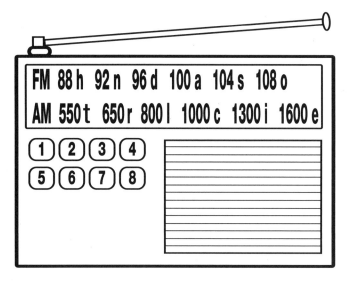

FM 88 h 92 n 96 d 100 a 104 s 108 o
AM 550 t 650 r 800 l 1000 c 1300 i 1600 e

T h e y   w e r e
am550 fm88 am1600   am1600 am650 am1600

p r a y i n g a n d
am650 fm100 am1300 fm92   fm100 fm92 fm96

s i n g i n g
fm104 am1300 fm92 am1300 fm92

h ym n s t o
fm88   fm92 fm104   am550 fm108

G o d . (from Acts 10:25)
fm108 fm96

A v i o l e n t   e a r t h qu a k e
fm100   am1300 fm108 am800 am1600 fm92 am550   am1600 fm100 am650 am550 fm88   fm100 am1600

c a u s e d t h e
am1000 fm100 fm104 am1600 fm96   am550 fm88 am1600

f o u n d a t i o n s   o f t h e
fm108 fm92 fm96 fm100 am550 am1300 fm108 fm92 fm104   fm108   am550 fm88 am1600

p r i s o n t o   s h a k e a n d
am650 am1300 fm104 fm108 fm92   am550 fm108   fm104 fm88 fm100 am1600   fm100 fm92 fm96

a l l   t h e p r i s o n
fm100 am800 am800   am550 fm88 am1600   am650 am1300 fm104 fm108 fm92

d o o r s o p e n e d a n d
fm96 fm108 fm108 am650 fm104   fm108 am1600 fm92 am1600 fm96   fm100 fm92 fm96

e v e ry b o dy's   c h a i n s
am1600 am1600 am650 fm108 fm96 fm104   am1000 fm88 fm100 am1300 fm92 fm104

c a m e l o o s e . (from Acts 10:26)
am1000 fm100 am1600   am800 fm108 fm108 fm104 am1600

All in a Day's Work
Acts 18:1-4, 18-21

Priscilla was Aquila's wife. The Bible says she helped her husband in their business. She also helped Paul share the gospel. What type of business did Priscilla and Aquila own? Cross out all the letters that are shown five times or more. Unscramble the remaining letters to find the answer.

```
G  J  V  P  D  H  C  V  J  T
A  D  F  N  G  L  B  H  G  F
H  J  V  P  B  F  Q  T  J  C
P  F  B  D  E  Q  K  J  Q  D
F  Q  B  V  H  L  B  H  C  P
E  C  L  V  C  M  H  D  Q  R
G  L  V  B  L  F  P  S  G  L
```

__ __ __ __ __ __ __ __ __ __

(from Acts 18:1-3)

83

All in a Day's Work

Answer

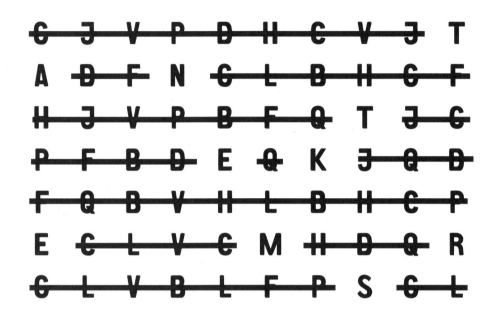

~~C J V P D H C V J~~ T
A ~~D F N C L B H C F~~
~~H J V P B F Q T J C~~
~~P F B D~~ E ~~Q~~ K ~~J Q D~~
~~F Q B V H L B H C P~~
E ~~C L V C~~ M ~~H D Q~~ R
~~C L V B L F P~~ S ~~C L~~

T E N T M A K E R S

(from Acts 18:1-3)

84

The Promised Seal
Ephesians 1:3-14

When you accept Christ as your Savior, you are marked with an "inner seal." This seal from God means that you will one day live with Him in heaven forever. Find the name of this promised seal (which is also a person) and the guarantee of eternal life with God. Begin at the bottom with the letter H. Work from right to left, writing every other letter to find the answer.

```
Y U R V O K L L G M S R I S H T F V O X E A S B I C A S R T P U E Y H Z T
A O B T F N T O W I Y S J S N E N S P S Q O U P W S Y D Z O D G E E R R
V A W O Y H D W C E E S S O X H I T O F G O O N L O F I G T H P Q M P E O
D E E N R I E J H G T M L R I Y T H N R U Q E N C M N K A J T I I J R B E A
H C N D I F R G U H O K G L N Q I Z E G E S T T N H A I R K A L U Z G W T
U I V S Q O O P L E P D Q A F S U I V O F H G W M T N I O R J I Y P X S V Y
T L S O P H N D K E M S J I O M B O E R W P X E Y H D T E L P A Q E V S
W A X H A T D I E W F M I I N H C N D I Z D A E B K O R R A S M T E U R Y
E Z W B U C O G Y H D A E B V C E D I E L F E H B H G I N J I K V L A M Ⓗ
```

_____

_____

_____

– Ephesians 1:13b-14

85

The Promised Seal

Answer

Y U R V O K L L G M S R I S H T F V O X E A S B I C A S R T P U E Y H Z T
A O B T F N T O W I Y S J S N E N S P S Q O U P W S Y D Z O D G E E R R
V A W O Y H D W C E E S S O X H I T O F G O O N L O F I G T H P Q M P E O
D E E N R I E J H G T M L R I Y T H N R U Q E N C M N K A J T I I J R B E A
H C N D I F R G U H O K G L N Q I Z E G E S T T N H A I R K A L U Z G W T
U I V S Q O O P L E P D Q A F S U I V O F H G W M T N I O R J I Y P X S V Y
T L S O P H N D K E M S J I O M B O E R W P X E Y H D T E L P A Q E V S
W A X H A T D I E W F M I I N H C N D I Z D A E B K O R R A S M T E U R Y
E Z W B U C O G Y H D A E B V C E D I E L F E H B H G I N J I K V L A M (H)

Having believed, you were marked in him with a seal, the promised Holy

Spirit, who is a deposit guaranteeing our inheritance until the redemption

of those who are God's possession - to the praise of his glory.

- Ephesians 1:13b-14

A Busy Man
Colossians 4:14

Luke was a character in the New Testament. He is credited with writing two books of the Bible; he also had another profession, and he is mentioned in several of Paul's letters to the various churches in the Bible. Add or subtract the letters as directed to answer the following questions. Individual words are separated by a "/."

1. What was Luke to Paul?

SPRAY - SPRY / SWIFT - SWIT + SHE - SH + LITTLE - LITTE + SMALL - SMAL + SPOON - SPON + FLOWER - FLOER / SHOWER - SHOER + FLOAT - FLAT + RACE - ACE + SKIM - SIM + ENVELOPE - ENVLOPE + SCORE - SCOE

_____

2. What two books of the Bible did Luke write?

BLANKET - BANKET + ASTOUND - ASTOND + SKILL - SILL + ELEVATE - ELEVAT _____

SCATTER - SCTTER + CRACKERS - CRAKERS + PATIENCE - PAIENCE + HESITATE - HEITATE _____

3. What was his other profession?

PLAYGROUND - PLAYGROUN + SPONSOR - SPONSR + GUIDANCE - GUIDANE + PRETEND - PREEND + VICTORIOUS - VICTORIUS + PERSONALITY - PESONALITY_____

(from Colossians 4:14)

A Busy Man

Answer

1. What was Luke to Paul?

SPRAY - SPRY / SWIFT - SWIT + SHE - SH + LITTLE - LITTE +

SMALL - SMAL + SPOON - SPON + FLOWER - FLOER / SHOWER

- SHOER + FLOAT - FLAT + RACE - ACE + SKIM - SIM + ENVELO

PE - ENVLOPE + SCORE - SCOE

A fellow worker

2. What two books of the Bible did Luke write?

BLANKET - BANKET + ASTOUND - ASTOND + SKILL - SILL +

ELEVATE - ELEVAT   Luke

SCATTER - SCTTER + CRACKERS - CRAKERS + PATIENCE -

PAIENCE + HESITATE - HEITATE   Acts

3. What was his other profession?

PLAYGROUND - PLAYGROUN + SPONSOR - SPONSR +

GUIDANCE - GUIDANE + PRETEND - PREEND + VICTORIOUS

- VICTORIUS + PERSONALITY - PESONALITY   Doctor

(from Colossians 4:14)

Run from Evil
1 Timothy 6:11-16

Timothy became a worker for Christ because he heard Paul's teachings about Jesus. Paul told Timothy to run from all that was evil and instead pursue other things. To find the things Paul encouraged Timothy to pursue, use the graph to find each letter. Then subtract six letters from the one given.

▬ ▬

	6	7	8	9
1	Z	Y	G	L
2	R	N	X	D
3	K	A	C	M
4	J	O	R	T
5	B	U	I	Z

Example: 3/6 = K - 6 = E

A B C D E F G H I J K L M N O P Q R S T U V W X Y Z

▬ ▬

‾‾ ‾‾ ‾‾ ‾‾ ‾‾ ‾‾ ‾‾ ‾‾ ‾‾ ‾‾ ‾‾ ‾‾ ‾‾
2/8 4/7 3/9 2/7 1/6 3/6 5/7 3/7 1/7 4/9 3/6 1/7 1/7

‾‾ ‾‾ ‾‾ ‾‾ ‾‾ ‾‾ ‾‾ ‾‾ ‾‾   ‾‾ ‾‾ ‾‾ ‾‾ ‾‾
3/9 5/7 4/6 2/6 4/7 4/9 3/6 1/7 1/7   1/9 1/8 4/7 1/6 2/7

‾‾ ‾‾ ‾‾ ‾‾   ‾‾ ‾‾ ‾‾ ‾‾ ‾‾ ‾‾ ‾‾ ‾‾ ‾‾
2/6 5/7 5/6 3/6   3/6 4/9 4/6 3/7 2/8 1/8 4/9 5/8 3/6

‾‾ ‾‾ ‾‾ ‾‾ ‾‾ ‾‾ ‾‾ ‾‾ ‾‾ ‾‾
3/9 3/6 4/9 1/6 2/6 3/6 4/9 3/6 1/7 1/7

‾‾ ‾‾ ‾‾   ‾‾ ‾‾
1/8 4/9 4/6   1/6 5/7

‾‾ ‾‾ ‾‾ ‾‾ ‾‾   ‾‾ ‾‾ ‾‾   ‾‾ ‾‾ ‾‾ ‾‾   ‾‾ ‾‾ ‾‾ ‾‾ ‾‾
1/9 4/7 3/9 2/7 1/6   1/6 2/7 3/6   3/9 5/7 5/7 4/6   1/9 4/7 3/9 2/7 1/6

(from 1 Timothy 6:11-12a)

‾‾ ‾‾   ‾‾ ‾‾ ‾‾   ‾‾ ‾‾ ‾‾ ‾‾ ‾‾
5/7 1/9   1/6 2/7 3/6   1/9 1/8 4/7 1/6 2/7

89

Run from Evil

Answer

1	Z	Y	G	L
2	R	N	X	D
3	K	A	C	M
4	J	O	R	T
5	B	U	I	Z
	6	7	8	9

A B C D E F G H I J K L M N O P Q R S T U V W X Y Z

R i g h t e o u s n e s s
2/8 4/7 3/9 2/7 1/6 3/6 5/7 3/7 1/7 4/9 3/6 1/7 1/7

G o d l i n e s s   f a i t h
3/9 5/7 4/6 2/6 4/7 4/9 3/6 1/7 1/7   1/9 1/8 4/7 1/6 2/7

l o v e   e n d u r a n c e
2/6 5/7 5/6 3/6   3/6 4/9 4/6 3/7 2/8 1/8 4/9 5/8 3/6

g e n t l e n e s s
3/9 3/6 4/9 1/6 2/6 3/6 4/9 3/6 1/7 1/7

a n d   t o
1/8 4/9 4/6   1/6 5/7

f i g h t t h e g o o d f i g h t
1/9 4/7 3/9 2/7 1/6 1/6 2/7 3/6 3/9 5/7 5/7 4/6 1/9 4/7 3/9 2/7 1/6

o f t h e f a i t h   **(from 1 Timothy 6:11-12a)**
5/7 1/9 1/6 2/7 3/6 1/9 1/8 4/7 1/6 2/7

Enoch's Faith

Hebrews 11:1-6

Enoch was an Old Testament figure who was known to "walk with God." The writer of Hebrews used Enoch's faith as an example of what ours should be. Because of his faith, Enoch experienced something incredible. To find out what it was, begin figuring out the puzzle by changing the first letter given by subtracting two (example: if the letter is L, then change it to J). Leave any other letters unchanged. Then change the last letter given in each word (if more than one is given) by adding three (example: if the last letter is M, change it to P). Then place the missing vowels in each remaining blank using A, E, I, O, U and Y.

A B C D E F G H I J K L M N O P Q R S T U V W X Y Z

D__ h___te __p__ce y__p v__k__k hr__j vh__p

_____

n__c__, u__ vh__q j__ f__a p__q __zp__r___nz__

_____

f___te; j__ e___la p__q d__ h___na, d__c___p__

_____

i__a j__a v__k__k j__j __y___. H__o d__f__o__ j__

_____

y__p v__k__k, j__ y__p e__mm__nd__a __u __p__

_____

ye__ rl___s__a i__a.

_____ – Hebrews 11:5

91

Enoch's Faith

Answer

A B C D E F G H I J K L M N O P Q R S T U V W X Y Z

D__ h___te __p__ce y__p v__k_k hr__j vh__p

By faith Enoch was taken from this

n__c_, u__ vh__q j__ f__a p__q __zp__r___nz__

life, so that he did not experience

f___te; j__ e___la p__q d__ h___na, d__c__p__

death; he could not be found, because

i__a j__a v__k_k j__j __y__. H__o d__f__o__ j__

God had taken him away. For before he

y__p v__k_k, j__ y__p e__mm__nd__a __u __p__

was taken, he was commended as one

ye__ rl___s__a i__a.

who pleased God.   – Hebrews 11:5

92

It's All About Anger
James 1:19-21

James, a disciple of Jesus, wrote the book called "James" in the New Testament. His book deals with how to live as a Christian – not always an easy task! Unscramble each word in the word bank. Then put the words in the correct spaces at the bottom to find James' teachings on anger.

erobthrs	isletn	losw	rngae	kpsea	nverEyoe
___	___	___	___	___	___
hte	anms	odes	ngary	lwso	fo
___	___	___	___	___	___
keta	sresdie	htat	utigerhos	ofr	eadr
___	___	___	___	___	___
dsolhu	yM	ot	eecbom	ot	nda
___	___	___	___	___	___
ribng	otn	file	tboau	oGd	eb
___	___	___	___	___	___
onte	hits	uiqck	ot		
___	___	___	___		

__ __   __ __ a __   __ __ __ __ h __ __ __,   t__ __ __

__ __ __ e __   __ __   __ __ __ s: __ v __ __ __ __ __ __ __

__ __ __ __ l __   __ __   __ __ __ __ k   __ __   __ __ __ __ __ __ n,

s__ __ __   __ __   p__ __ __   __ n__   __ __ o __   __ __

__ __ c __ __ __   __ n __ __ __,   __ __ r   m __ __ __ ' __

__ __ __ e __   d __ __ __   __ __ t   __ r __ __ __   __ __ __ u __

t __ __   __ __ __ h __ __ __ __   l __ __ __   __ __ __ t

G __ __   __ __ __ __ __ r __ __.   – James 1:19-20

93

It's All About Anger

Answer

erobthrs	isletn	losw	rngae	kpsea	nverEyoe
brothers	listen	slow	anger	speak	Everyone
hte	**anms**	**odes**	**ngary**	**lwso**	**fo**
the	man's	does	angry	slow	of
keta	**sresdie**	**htat**	**utigerhos**	**ofr**	**eadr**
take	desires	that	righteous	for	read
dsolhu	**yM**	**ot**	**eecbom**	**ot**	**nda**
should	My	to	become	to	and
ribng	**otn**	**file**	**tboau**	**oGd**	**eb**
bring	not	life	about	God	be
onte	**hits**	**uiqck**	**ot**		
note	this	quick	to		

My dear brothers, take note of this: Everyone should be quick to listen, slow to speak and slow to become angry, for man's anger does not bring about the righteous life that God desires. **– James 1:19-20**

No Darkness
1 John 1:5-7

John, one of Jesus' disciples, wrote the Gospel of John and the three epistles of John, all of which are in the Bible. In the first chapter of 1 John, he emphasizes one message in particular. What is this message? Each word in the word bank (except the two-letter words) has a single letter missing. Fill in the missing letters, then place the words on the correct lines to find the important message.

1. t__e
2. li__ht
3. wi__h
4. Go__
5. __he
6. hi__
7. lig__t
8. t__ere
9. fel__owship
10. bloo__
11. puri__ies
12. is
13. is
14. dark__ess
15. wa__k
16. f__om
17. si__
18. __nd
19. al__
20. in
21. at
22. is
23. no
24. we
25. anot__er
26. S__n
27. if
28. on__
29. ha__e
30. Je__us
31. us
32. th__
33. we
34. in
35. of
36. ligh__
37. __ll
38. in
39. hi__
40. as
41. he

__ __ __ ; __ __ __ __ __ __ __
4   22   7   20   6   8   13 23 14

__ __ . . . . __ __ __ __ __ __ , __
21 19   27   24 15 34 1   36   40

__ __ __ __ __ , __ __ __
41 12 38 5   2   33 29 9

__ __ __ , __ __ __ __
3   28 25   18 32 10 35

__ , __ __ , __ __ __ __ .
30   39 26   11 31 16 37 17

- 1 John 1:5b, 7

No Darkness

Answer

1. t__h__e   2. li__g__ht   3. wi__t__h   4. Go__d__   5. __t__he   6. hi__m__

7. lig__h__t   8. t__h__ere   9. fel__l__owship   10. bloo__d__   11. puri__f__ies   12. is

13. is   14. dark__n__ess   15. wa__l__k   16. f__r__om   17. si__n__   18. __a__nd

19. al__l__   20. in   21. at   22. is   23. no   24. we

25. anot__h__er   26. S__o__n   27. if   28. on__e__   29. ha__v__e   30. Je__s__us

31. us   32. th__e__   33. we   34. in   35. of   36. ligh__t__

37. __a__ll   38. in   39. hi__s__   40. as   41. he

God   is   light;   in   him   there   is   no   darkness
 4   22   7   20   6   8   13   23   14

at   all ....   If   we   walk   in   the   light,   as
21   19   27   24   15   34   1   36   40

he   is   in   the   light,   we   have   fellowship
41   12   38   5   2   33   29   9

with   one   another,   and   the   blood   of
 3   28   25   18   32   10   35

Jesus,   his   Son ,   purifies   us   from   all   sin .
 30   39   26   11   31   16   37   17

— 1 John 1:5b, 7

96